GOD'S AN ARTIST AND
YOU'RE A MASTERPIECE

GOD'S AN ARTIST AND YOU'RE A MASTERPIECE

The Mind-Boggling Science of an Awesome Creator

LORRAINE PETERSON

Kregel
Publications

God's an Artist and You're a Masterpiece: The Mind-Boggling Science of an Awesome Creator

© 2004 by Lorraine Peterson

Published by Kregel Publications, P.O. Box 2607, Grand Rapids, MI 49501.

Cover design: John M. Lucas

ISBN   0-8254-3467-x

Printed in the United States of America

04 05 06 07 08 / 5 4 3 2 1

CONTENTS

PREFACE

Anne's* idea of students' rights differed drastically from mine. As a high school teacher, I explained, "I believe that all students must have the right to learn, and no one should be given liberties that would prevent another from gaining knowledge." But I agreed with Anne about one particular student right: A student should never be put down or belittled.

I shocked her, though, by saying, "The cruelest thing that could be done to students is to teach them that everything evolved from matter, chance, and time."

The theory of evolution leaves young people with no moral compass, no one to pray to, and no hope. If teens decide that the first pages of Genesis are pure myth, they can then conclude that the God of the Bible doesn't exist. In doing so, a teen forfeits the belief that

- his or her life is intrinsically valuable solely because God planned it;
- God loves each person unconditionally;
- life has meaning beyond the now;
- help and guidance are available from Someone who knows everything and has all power;
- it's possible to accept God's forgiveness and be sure of heaven.

No amount of self-esteem indoctrination can replace these losses.

A person doesn't need an advanced degree in science to think

---

* Name changed to protect privacy

rationally about how our universe came into being. But if the study of science becomes only the learning of terms, the presenting of unproven theories as fact, the classification of species, and the memorizing of certain physical laws, it's easy to miss out on the wonders found in God's fantastic universe. *God's an Artist and You're a Masterpiece* shows some of the marvels of creation that point to intelligent design and that inspire awe and worship of the Creator. It would be a shame to miss out on the celebration described in Psalm 69:34: "Let heaven and earth praise him, the seas and all that move in them."

The case for intelligent design is often presented theoretically or by citing only a couple of pieces of evidence. *God's an Artist and You're a Masterpiece* presents a panorama of fascinating facts and phenomena in the natural world. These things must be explained as either a product of preexistent matter—assisted by time and chance —or of intelligent design.

Deciding between these two explanations relates to choices about how you live your daily life. So besides offering rational evidence for Creation, *God's an Artist and You're a Masterpiece* presents narratives that show that the price of rejecting God as the Creator is great—in terms of personal happiness, purpose for living, and the ability to genuinely care about people who are hard to love.

At the foundation of all cultural beliefs lies one question: Did God make the universe? If He didn't, all views are equally valid and absolute truth doesn't exist. If He didn't, life consists only of molecules, so abortion and assisted suicide are perfectly acceptable. If He didn't, greed, cheating, and lying can't be termed sin. If He didn't, then anything goes—every kind of sex is acceptable, marriage can be broadly defined, right and wrong can change every decade, and public opinion polls can determine truth.

If the God of the Bible doesn't exist, there's nothing to live for, and people are forced to create their own meaning in life—by accumulating more and more stuff, or by stepping on others to get ahead, or by insisting that their rights never be offended in any way, or by getting everyone to like them, or by being publicly recognized for making contributions to society.

If there is no heavenly Father who has prepared a place in heaven for those who know Him, failure is frustration with no place to go. If there is no God who fits the description given in the Bible, all of today's politically correct conclusions are extremely logical.

If, on the other hand, one believes that God created the world with a purpose, and that He is revealed in the Bible and through His Son Jesus Christ, then one's worldview changes. The sanctity of human life, moral responsibility as defined in Scripture, the awareness that everything contrary to the will of God is sin, the value of each person regardless of achievement or quality of life, and living with hope for eternity become part of that worldview.

With these choices before us, it's like we're standing with Elijah on Mount Carmel. But instead of deciding whether to worship God or the idol Baal, we must decide whether to believe that the God described in the Bible actually created the heavens and the earth, or to believe that the universe came about by forces of blind chance. The choice we make will determine how we live and how we interpret what is happening around us.

God's an Artist and You're a Masterpiece differs from other books that address the intelligent design of the universe. Some of those books have been written by Bible scholars—who know Hebrew well enough to distinguish subtle word meanings. Other such books have been written by creation scientists—who enjoy investigating how nature works and proposing ideas on how God originated the universe and the things in it. Because their books debate God's methods of creation and how long it took Him, some of their theories may be changed by new discoveries.

God's an Artist and You're a Masterpiece seeks solely to demonstrate that the universe came into existence as a result of an intelligent Designer. It points out how that Designer's character is reflected in the things He made—and shows how that fact should influence your life.

Remember, "science is a train that is always moving," but God's Word "is eternal; it stands firm in the heavens" (Ps. 119:89).

ACKNOWLEDGMENTS

My thanks to my family and friends, who have supported me in writing this book and have prayed for me during the process. During my visit to Alaska, my niece Beth and my nephew Michael aided me in my research by checking out books for me on their library cards.

I was encouraged, too, by the positive reaction when I used some of the material from *God's an Artist and You're a Masterpiece* to teach the teen Bible club that meets at my apartment in Juarez, Mexico—in spite of the fact that my science vocabulary in Spanish leaves a lot to be desired!

A very special thanks goes to Paul Nyhuis, without whose assistance this book wouldn't have become reality. Paul graduated from Wheaton College with a B.S. in mathematics and earned his master's degree in physics from the University of Minnesota. He has taught physics and astronomy at the college level for thirty-five years. Paul proofread this manuscript, helped me find information, did calculations to put some facts in terms that teens can relate to, and made many valuable suggestions.

My appreciation also goes to Michael J. Minnima, who taught with me at Edison High School in Minneapolis, for carefully reading this manuscript. Mike has an M.S. and has won two awards from the American Chemical Society, plus he also received a National Presidential Award in 1996. Because he has taught high school science for thirty-three years, he not only checked the technical side of this book, he also offered insights into the thinking and vocabulary of today's American teens.

I'm extremely grateful to Dr. Donald A. Bierle, who holds a Ph.D. from the University of South Dakota with a major in zoology and a minor in botany, plus an M.A. from Denver Seminary. His invaluable help greatly improved the accuracy of large sections of this manuscript. He is president of Faith Studies International, and his book, *Surprised by Faith,* is endorsed by Billy Graham and D. James Kennedy.[1]

Dr. Jeff Michell has my thanks for reviewing the medical facts that are included in this book. He is a family physician who is the medical director of Fairview Cedar Ridge Clinic in Apple Valley, Minnesota.

Dr. Kevin Peterson not only gave input on the areas that touched the medical field—for which I thank him—but he also read the manuscript with his teenagers. A big thanks to Joe, Nick, Bill, and Nathan for their suggestions that helped the book become more teen-friendly.

Most of all, I praise God for His incredible faithfulness and the many answers to prayer that are represented by this book.

1

MADE TO ORDER

DID YOU KNOW?

Life, especially advanced life, could not exist on planet Earth if any of these conditions existed:
- if the Earth rotated 4 percent slower
- if the Earth rotated 4 percent faster
- if the Earth were 2 to 5 percent farther from the sun
- if the Earth were 2 to 5 percent closer to the sun
- if the Earth had more than one moon
- if the Earth had a larger moon*
- if the Earth had a smaller moon
- if the Earth were larger
- if the Earth were smaller
- if the Earth had a thinner crust
- if the Earth had a thicker crust
- if the Earth's ozone layer were thicker or thinner[1]
- if the size and shape of our galaxy were markedly different
- if our galaxy were too close to neighboring galaxies[2]
- if the Earth's sun were either larger or smaller[3]
- if the Earth's oxygen-to-nitrogen ratio were less or greater

---

* Here, larger and smaller refer to weight, not volume. The technical term is *mass*. The variations referred to by *faster, slower, larger, smaller, thinner, thicker, closer, farther, less,* and *greater* range from 2–10 percent.

- if the Earth's atmosphere had a greater or lesser level of carbon dioxide
- if the quantity of oxygen in Earth's atmosphere were less or greater
- if Earth had a greater or smaller ocean-to-continent ratio[4]
- if the Earth's atmospheric pressure were too intense or not intense enough
- if Jupiter were closer to or farther from the Earth
- if Jupiter were larger or smaller
- if too much land mass were concentrated in the Earth's southern hemisphere[5]
- if a greater or smaller quantity of iron were in the Earth's oceans and soils[6]

This list could go on and on. As time passes, scientists find more and more evidence that Earth is especially designed for physical life. As of 2001, a list of 123 fine-tuned conditions in our solar system had been identified that make human existence on our planet possible.[7]

It would prove an amazing coincidence if all these conditions for life on this planet came about by chance. It's actually easier to believe that God created the universe just for you—as well as for all the other people who have lived or will live on Earth.

Look again at the facts. I think you'll agree that God is cheering for you—because He made a universe for you. Both His physical laws and His moral laws are designed to protect you and to help you have a life worth living.

DOES IT MATTER?

Kevin's mother was religious, but she was also demanding and severe. His church taught him that he'd better obey all kinds of rules and regulations or God would zap him. Kevin tried to get along with his mother and also to conform to what his church said, but he hated every minute of it.

Then Ms. Carson, his biology teacher, offered him a way out. "It's a fact," she stated, "that everything around us arose from natural causes. A simple cell, like an amoeba, started everything. And billions of mutations later, here we are. Some people are too cowardly to face the truth that our universe, and we ourselves, are accidents, and matter is all that there is."

Kevin listened intently. *If there's no God,* he thought, *I can do whatever I wish.* He decided he'd lie to his mother and live a double life.

If Kevin didn't feel like studying, he made cheat sheets. Because he was a good student, no one even suspected him. He started asking out pretty girls just to impress his friends. And he soon learned how to live in the fast lane.

Daring by nature, Kevin joined a motorcycle gang. He found the races that his gang took part in held the most appeal. But he soon learned that drinking, drugs, and intimidating people were part of that lifestyle package.

Kevin figured, "If death means the end of existence, I'll live it up while I'm young." Getting old would be too boring. He won most races and took a lot of chances—until the day he crashed into an oak tree. Much worse than the terrible pain and the hospital confinement was the doctor's verdict: "I'm sorry, Kevin, but you'll never walk again."

VITAL INFORMATION

Most people don't consider themselves smart enough to improve upon the natural laws of the universe, yet many think nothing of changing God's moral principles. Lots of individuals, like Kevin, like to call their own shots and make up their own rules, declaring "Anything goes!"

Others, like the rule makers in Kevin's church, invent all kinds of regulations, proclaiming them to be straight from God Himself. It's important, then, that you check out the biblical basis for anyone's "dos and don'ts" before you accept them as coming from the Lord. You should, in fact, find out what the Bible says before you believe *anything.*

One of the Devil's oldest lies is that God is mean and doesn't want you to have any fun. To prove it, human-imposed rules are usually cited—rules that have nothing to do with God's commandments.

Remember that God's physical laws exist in order to give you the best possible place to live. The design in the creation of a universe, galaxy, and planet that are exactly right for you shows that God cares, and that He has your best interests in mind. His moral laws—not always the same as prohibitions imposed by people—are meant to protect you, because God says you are extremely valuable. God really is good, and what He does is good.

IF KEVIN MEETS CHRISTIANS WHO CARE, THIS COULD BE THE NEXT CHAPTER IN HIS LIFE . . .

After a long rehabilitation, Kevin left the hospital in a wheelchair. Devastated and feeling that he had nothing to live for, he contemplated suicide. Although his mother said nothing directly, Kevin sensed that she thought God was punishing him for disobeying the church's rules.

Returning to school in a wheelchair was a nightmare. His old friends had abandoned him after the accident, and the majority of the staff and students didn't know what to say to him. Most regarded him as a curiosity. A couple of teachers were extra nice to him so, since there was nothing else he could do, he studied hard and got some good grades. But his heart wasn't in it.

If death really means oblivion, Kevin thought, *it sounds like my best option.* Only the fear that God might really exist kept him from slashing his wrists.

The one bright spot in that first month was social studies class. Kevin parked his wheelchair next to Kayla's seat at the end of the front row. She always greeted him with a smile and asked how he was doing.

She introduced him to Lanny, who was also in their class. Lanny invited Kevin to eat lunch with Kayla and their group of friends. Not wanting to alienate the only people who seemed to care about him, Kevin accepted. He was shocked when they all bowed their heads for prayer before eating. They seemed like they really wanted to pray, without anyone telling them they had to.

Lanny and Kayla introduced him to the rest of their group, and everyone was friendly and kind. Kevin felt relaxed around them, so he ate with them almost every day. They talked about God, prayer, church, and plans for their high school Bible club as if those things were the most important parts of their lives.

Yet they were fun to be around. Lanny was always cracking jokes. And one day Hugh placed a rubber cockroach on top of Kayla's hamburger. Her scream attracted a lot of attention, and she blushed a bright red. But she was a good sport about it.

Still, when the group invited Kevin to Bible club, he refused. But they didn't push or make a big deal about it. They just kept loving him and accepting him.

He found out that Jessica had been part of the group for only six months. One day she sat next to Kevin at lunch, and he heard her tell Debbie, "I'll have to miss Bible study tonight. I can't find a babysitter."

"You have a kid?" Kevin asked.

"Yes," said Jessica. "Before I received Jesus as my Savior I was a drug addict. In fact, I broke almost all of God's commandments." Jessica spoke in a matter-of-fact way. "I didn't know that God made rules because He loves me and wants to protect me. Now I know why God prohibits sex before marriage . . . and why He doesn't want me to steal or to abuse my body with things like drugs. All of those things caused me a lot of pain. But now that I know Jesus, my life is happy, and I realize that He has a great plan for my life."

Kevin didn't say anything, but he was impressed. Jessica was beautiful, fun-loving, confident, and intelligent. And she was also a very caring person. Yet neither she nor her friends followed all the rules that his mother insisted upon—or the dress code imposed by her church.

What they had was genuine, and it made them different from any friends he'd ever had. He'd known girls who were immoral and used drugs. They were hardened and almost unfeeling. He never would have guessed that Jessica had once been like that.

Mario invited the whole group to his birthday party and even arranged special transportation for Kevin. After the party, Kevin had to admit that these kids had more fun—even without depending upon any artificial high—than any of the kids at the parties he used to attend.

The group continued to include him in their social activities, saying, "When you want to come to Bible study with us, just let us know."

Pete became Kevin's closest friend. Quiet and unassuming, Pete had a special gift for meeting the needs of hurting people. He sat *down* to talk to Kevin, even when everyone else was standing. He made sure that Kevin was the scorekeeper when they played volleyball, and tried to include Kevin in other activities. Pete picked up Kevin for athletic events at school and saw that he got a ride when they all went out for pizza.

Little by little, Kevin began to confide in Pete, asking him questions about God. Kevin couldn't believe all the scientific information Pete had stored in his head. The way Pete connected all that information with God seemed so natural.

Kevin began to think that Someone superintelligent was, in fact, behind the universe. He began to see the Lord's hand in creation as well as in the changed lives of his friends. He started to realize that talking about God was one thing, but really knowing Him and reflecting His love was quite another.

Maybe you, like Kevin, have decided to give up on God or believe that He just doesn't exist. You've likely seen a lot of hypocrisy, or someone from a church has deeply hurt you. In light of all the Creator has done to make a special planet for you to live on, you may wish to reconsider.

ACTION STEPS FOR FINDING OUT WHAT GOD IS REALLY LIKE

1. Carefully consider all alternatives. If the God of the Bible doesn't exist, who or what will you believe in?
2. Read Isaiah 40–46 and write down everything you learn about God.
3. Ask yourself, "Is it fair to judge God by what other people say about Him— especially if those people have been hurt by hypo-

crites, or they want to do whatever they wish without a guilty conscience?"

4. Try to find a person who really seems to know the God of the Bible and interview him or her.

WORDS TO LIVE BY

> By wisdom the LORD laid the earth's foundations,
>> by understanding he set the heavens in place;
> by his knowledge the deeps were divided,
>> and the clouds let drop the dew.
>
> — Proverbs 3:19–20

> The law of the LORD is perfect,
>> reviving the soul.
> The statutes of the LORD are trustworthy,
>> making wise the simple.
> The precepts of the LORD are right,
>> giving joy to the heart.
> The commands of the LORD are radiant,
>> giving light to the eyes.
>
> — Psalm 19:7–8

2

UNDER CONTROL

On July 22, 2009, there will be a total solar eclipse that will last six minutes and thirty-nine seconds. It will be seen in Nepal, Burma, and China, and it will be the longest eclipse of the twenty-first century.

A total solar eclipse won't occur in the United States until August 21, 2017, and will be over in two minutes and forty seconds. It will be visible in Oregon, Idaho, Nebraska, Missouri, Illinois, Tennessee, North Carolina, and South Carolina.

The longest total eclipse in recorded history lasted seven minutes and twenty-eight seconds, and it took place on June 15, 744 B.C.

A total eclipse occurs when the moon completely covers the sun. How can that happen since the sun is four hundred times the diameter of the moon? Because the sun is about four hundred times farther away from the Earth than the moon is, the two appear about the same size in the sky. When the Earth's orbit around the sun and the moon's orbit around the Earth intersect—usually twice in 346.62 days—an eclipse occurs.

Typically a solar eclipse occurs at new moon twice a year. Two partial eclipses, though, within a month of each other are possible. The maximum number of solar eclipses possible in a year is five—four partial and one central.[1] In 2000, four partial solar eclipses occurred. Five solar eclipses occurred in 1935, and five will occur again in 2206.[2]

The heavenly rhythm is so accurate that, with rare exceptions, a solar eclipse can be predicted by adding eighteen years and eleven days to the date of any previous solar eclipse. It's also possible to calculate backwards and know that Jerusalem experienced an eclipse on July 4, 336 B.C. London experienced one on October 29, 878 A.D.[3]

If the predictable movement found in space came from material that just *happened* to have always been there, and that *accidentally* and *spontaneously* organized itself in such a precise way, you could expect, too, that your room will clean itself and that your homework assignments will miraculously be completed!

Realistically, we can be sure that an intelligent Creator orchestrated all this heavenly clockwork—and that He has every future event under His control.

DOES IT MATTER?

In silence, Tim watched the TV news with his parents. As usual the war on terrorism, homeland defense strategies, and fears of the unknown combined to have a depressing effect. It just didn't seem fair that a group of desperate people half a world away could ruin his future.

Tim dreamed of getting a baseball scholarship to a good college. He'd study to become a physical education teacher and coach, marry a beautiful girl who also liked to ski, and get a job in the mountains so they could go skiing every winter weekend.

But he wondered if he'd ever live to realize his plan. What if the military draft were reinstated and he was forced to fight—and maybe die—on foreign soil? What if the economy became so bad he couldn't afford to go to college? What if he and his friends and family became victims of biological warfare? Nothing seemed certain or secure.

VITAL INFORMATION

How should Tim face a future full of doubts and danger? How should you?

To plan a good life, be prepared for death, because if you're not afraid to die, you'll never be afraid to live.

The almighty God—who for thousands of years has planned solar eclipses down to the second—knows about every anthrax spore, every smallpox germ, every hijacking plan, and the intentions of each person who wants to commit suicide in order to kill innocent people. God is active in history. He has given humans free will, but it can only be exercised within the limits He imposes. And the Lord has already decided how the world will end and has told us about it in His Book.

IF TIM FACES HIS UNCERTAIN FUTURE
IN THE RIGHT WAY, THIS COULD BE
THE OUTCOME . . .

Things got worse for Tim before they got better. Two men suspected of being part of a terrorist plot had been arrested in their small city, so everyone was on edge. It was 1:17 P.M. and Tim was sitting in English class, deciding whether to fall asleep or draw cartoons in his notebook.

Suddenly a huge explosion shattered a couple of windows. Although he kept his cool on the outside, Tim was seized with panic. What if the school was the next building to be blown up?

I'm too young to die, he cried inwardly. He knew he wasn't prepared to face death.

Worried that the school building was a dangerous place to be, the janitor pulled the fire alarm and everyone filed out. Once outside they saw that, five blocks away, the plant that made lighter fluid for barbecue grills was in flames.

School officials then decided that the students would be safer inside, so they were instructed to return to classes. Teachers went through the motions of business as usual, but it was hard for them to be heard over the shriek of fire trucks and ambulance sirens, as well as the police captain giving instructions over a bullhorn at the fire scene.

Soon, word came over the school loudspeaker—the mayor had imposed a curfew. People who weren't medical personnel, members of the police or fire departments, or trained disaster volunteers who wore badges were to go directly to their homes and stay there until the curfew was lifted.

Tim spotted Cassie, the pretty redhead who lived on his street. "I'll walk you home," he offered. Actually he wasn't being a gentleman. He was frightened and anxious and didn't want to be alone.

As they walked, they talked about the explosion and fire.

"Pretty scary stuff, huh?" said Tim.

"Sure is," said Cassie. "I'm so glad God has everything under control. I used to be fearful and uptight. But since I accepted Jesus as my Savior, all that has changed. Now I know that I'll spend eternity with Him in heaven."

Tim could tell—Cassie truly was relaxed and unafraid.

"I've never been very religious," said Tim. "I figure that God—if He's real—should keep bad things from happening."

"If this world were all there is, you'd be right," Cassie said. "But God has more in store for us than our earthly life. He gave us souls that live forever, and forever is a long time. The purpose of this life is to get to know God so we can spend all eternity with Him. God allowed humans to have a free will and that has its downside—some people choose to do evil. But God uses all the bad stuff to accomplish a good purpose in the lives of those who love Him."

"You seem so confident and so unafraid of the future," said Tim. "Is that for real? Or are you just putting up a front?"

"My brother was killed in Iraq," said Cassie, looking straight at Tim. "I know what I'm talking about. I trust everything into God's hands. I'm planning to see my brother again—in heaven—and I'll introduce him to as many people as I can bring along with me."

"I wish I could be as sure about things as you are," said Tim as they approached Cassie's door.

"If you really mean that," Cassie said, "there's something you should read. I have to get inside because of the curfew . . . but wait just a second. I'll give you a booklet that'll tell you how to give your life to Christ."

After Cassie handed the booklet to Tim, he said good-bye, walked to the end of the block, and entered his empty house. Since both of his parents worked at a hospital, he didn't expect them home anytime soon. He turned on the TV and watched footage of the blaze, with the announcers saying, "We don't know that this is an act of terrorism, but every precaution is being taken."

Tim clicked off the television and thumbed through the little booklet that Cassie had given him. A few words caught his eye—*peace, security, love*—and Tim decided to read the whole thing.

When he finished, he thought for a moment, then he looked up at the ceiling and, for the first time in his life, Tim prayed: "God, if You're there, forgive my sins, come into my life, and give me peace."

Tim and Cassie had some long talks over the next couple of days—mostly by telephone. He started to realize that trusting God for every situation, for each day, and for the future was a decision—an act of will. He could choose to have confidence in God's love and His power, or he could continue to worry.

As it turned out, the explosion was due to the negligence of plant personnel. No one was killed, because all of those who worked in the area where the fire began were attending a recognition luncheon for a retiring worker. The injured would all recover. Everyone was relieved—and Tim was grateful that the next time something horrific happened, he wouldn't experience the terror of being unprepared to die.

You, too, can trust your eternal future to the God who has timed eclipses down to the second. What He says about salvation is the final word. Philosophical ideas change every decade. Because the predictions of psychics don't come true, their clients find neither peace nor hope. David told us, "The heavens declare the glory of God" (Ps. 19:1). When things get tough and worry tries to overwhelm you, look into the sky and remember that the God who spoke the whole universe into existence has enough power to change everything.

ACTION STEPS FOR FACING A NEW AND DANGEROUS WORLD

1. Make sure you've asked Jesus to forgive your sins and to rule your life.
2. Decide to thank God for His faithfulness every time you look at

. the sun or the moon, remembering that you can safely entrust
your future to Him.

3. Consciously put yourself in God's hands each morning before
   you start the day.
4. Resist the temptation to worry about things you can't control,
   telling God that you know He has the whole world covered.

WORDS TO LIVE BY

God is our refuge and strength,
  an ever-present help in trouble.
Therefore we will not fear, though the earth give way
  and the mountains fall into the heart of the sea. . . .
Be still, and know that I am God;
  I will be exalted among the nations,
  I will be exalted in the earth.
                                        —Psalm 46:1–2, 10

3

A DEFINITION FOR "GOOD"

Humans don't have all the superior capabilities. So if you believe that all living things evolved, becoming more and more advanced until humans ended up with top-notch abilities in all areas, think again.

Many owls can hear sounds ten times softer than humans can pick up.[1] Dogs can detect high-pitched sounds with frequencies up to forty-thousand vibrations per second while humans cannot hear sounds with more than twenty-thousand vibrations per second.

Animals beat out humans in the scent department too. A German shepherd or a bloodhound has 220 million smell cells compared to 5 million smell cells for humans.[2]

Think you have good eyesight? An eagle has eyes that are larger and six times sharper than those of a human.[3] Birds see everything at once—and in total focus—because their eyes are flat. The globe-shaped eyes of humans must adjust to varying distances.[4] And while humans have to pull out their shades to keep from squinting in the sun, seagulls have built-in sunglasses, actually droplets of reddish oil that shield the retina from the sun's blue light.[5]

The most gifted athletes alive can't top the abilities of even the smallest of creatures. A flea can jump one hundred times the height of its own body—the equivalent of a six-foot man jumping over a forty-story building—and can accelerate fifty times faster than the space shuttle.[6]

And the fastest moving animal is the peregrine falcon. Clocked at 217 miles per hour in a dive for prey,[7] it makes us look like snails. Well, not exactly—a snail moves at a rate of 0.000362005 miles per hour.[8]

While a person has six hundred muscles, a caterpillar has over two thousand.[9] An ant can lift fifty times its own weight, and a bee can handle three hundred times it own weight—equivalent to a human pulling a ten-ton trailer.[10]

Humans who like water sports will be interested to know that seals can dive to depths of up to 2,600 feet and stay under water for as long as two hours without coming up for air. The deepest dive on record—made by an elephant seal—is 4,135 feet. And unlike humans, they can resurface quickly without having to stop and let their bodies adjust to a different pressure.[11]

Do you like to travel? When humans take a long trip, we need maps to guide us and we take plenty of soda to quench our thirst. The Arctic tern, though, travels up to 22,000 miles a year without ever getting lost.[12] And the camel can keep going for three days, carrying a heavy load, without drinking a drop of water.[13]

The amazing abilities of these living creatures suggest variety and creativity, rather than an uninterrupted, chance progression that gave the highest life forms all the perks. Yet some people believe that all life is the end product of an evolutionary process that started from simple and moved to complex.

Life is often thought of as the product of energy, as though energy were capable of creative intelligence and possessed divine qualities. If your god is a blob of energy, maybe you should reconsider. Every living thing seems to scream, "Look, my Maker has tremendous intelligence, ingenuity, and imagination!" Consider the astounding complexity of even the simplest creature. Doesn't it stand to reason that the *real* God, who created everything, is more than a blob of energy, that He isn't limited to gradually improving the functions of living things, or restricted to endowing living things with gradually increasing complexity?

Stop and think. We conclude that even the most primitive line drawings are the result of intelligence and creative planning. So doesn't it follow that magnificent art is the result of creative *genius*? Is it logical, then, to believe that the magnificence of an eagle's eye or an owl's ear—or you, yourself—are the products of spontaneous energy?

DOES IT MATTER?

Brandon faced his parents.

"I can't believe it!" his mother screamed. "The first time we trust you to stay alone in the house for a weekend, you invited a girl to spend the night. Haven't we taught you good morals? What will the neighbors think?"

"Mother," Brandon responded coolly, leaning against the kitchen counter, "life is made up of experiences, and *all* of them are good. You have no right to judge me."

"I beg to differ," his father exploded. "What if the girl gets pregnant? You'll be responsible to support the baby. Didn't we send you to Sunday school so you could learn the Ten Commandments?"

"That's *your* truth," Brandon said, his voice smooth. "My truth is that God is an energy gestalt, and we're all part of God—and so is good and evil. My truth is that God judges no one for their actions, so neither should we. Besides, Sasha promised to get an abortion if the condom failed."

"I guess we're experiencing a generation chasm," said his mother, shaking her head.

"Nothing you say makes sense," his dad added. "You're forgetting all about the real world of sexually transmitted diseases ... and about post-abortion syndrome ... and breaking a girl's heart." Brandon's father left the kitchen in a huff, and Brandon went to his room.

VITAL INFORMATION

Your definition of God is terribly important because it defines "good." It affects everything you think and do. If you invent your own god, then that god becomes the creation and you've made yourself the creator. And the creator is always greater than the thing created.

When it comes to your beliefs about a god, your only choices are to

- accept a tradition or definition of a god that has been concocted by someone else;
- invent your own god;
- believe that a real God, who is higher than all He has made, actually exists and has revealed Himself to us in the Bible and through His Son Jesus Christ.

IF BRANDON REALLY THINKS THINGS THROUGH, THIS COULD BE HIS EXPERIENCE . . .

Brandon's theory about all experiences being good wasn't working out. Sasha did become pregnant, and her grandmother talked her into keeping the baby. Brandon's "solution" was to accuse her of breaking her promise, find a new girlfriend, and walk away. But he couldn't forget Sasha's heartbroken sobs. And because there were no secrets in his small town, he couldn't dodge the questions about his getting Sasha pregnant.

When the baby was born, everyone said he looked just like Brandon. Brandon had hoped to escape and attend college out of state. But his parents decided to use some of the money they'd saved for Brandon's college tuition to set up a trust fund for the care of Brandon and Sasha's baby. Such a gesture would, after all, improve their standing in the community and perhaps minimize the damage to the business owned by Brandon's father.

Brandon was bitterly disappointed that he wouldn't be able to attend a big-name college. So to cheer himself up, he and his best friend, Don, decided to spend their graduation money on a canoe trip.

Their spirits were high as they started down the river. It wandered through beautiful woodlands dotted with colorful spring flowers. At night, the stars—with no competition from street lights and neon signs—sparkled in a velvet sky. Every morning the birds gave them a free concert, and after a day of rain, they saw a breathtaking double rainbow.

Brandon was usually the life of the party, the practical joker, and the energetic leader who thought of exciting things to do. Don, with his quiet demeanor, was a good complement to Brandon. He silently followed along with whatever Brandon suggested. But now Brandon wished Don were more talkative.

Brandon had welcomed the chance to get away but, too late, he realized that canoeing gave him too much time to think about life— something he tried not to do. He was reminded of his chemistry teacher's words: "If you use the wrong formula, you won't get the results you're looking for." They seemed to describe how he was living.

Now he wondered about a lot of things. Especially the things his cousins had told him—and he'd believed—about God. He thought about the seminars he'd attended and the books he'd read at the suggestion of his cousins. He'd been taught that all experiences were good. *Ha!* thought Brandon. *Depends on your definition of* good. He was living a nightmare.

As he contemplated the wonders of nature, it seemed terribly unlikely that some energy gestalt created everything he saw. And if the seminars were right, why did he still, deep down, long for a personal God—One who would care about his problems and offer some help?

If he was part of God, like the books said, why did he feel guilty? Could it be that he really *needed* some rules to follow that would keep him from making more bad decisions?

He looked into the night sky. As the moon disappeared behind a cloud, he thought, *God, if You're up there and You really know everything, I need You.*

Perhaps you, like Brandon, should let the wonders of creation lead you to reflect on the Creator. What you see around you is awe inspiring. Every creature is unique and endowed with an individuality that we can appreciate. Each living thing has its own function and purpose. It's hard to believe, then, that each is merely the product of energy or natural forces. Behind all things there must exist a Being with personality, intelligence, and power.

That being is God. And God—not an energy gestalt, physical laws, or the process of evolution—placed within each of us a desire to connect meaningfully with our Creator. It's hard to pray to spontaneous energy and impossible to sense the love of an indifferent process! The good news is that God is real and God is personal. He actually is concerned about you. Why not join Brandon in admitting that you need His help.

ACTION STEPS FOR PROFILING CREATION

1. Read the following narrative and point out the presuppositions you find illogical:

    Two university professors from another universe crash-landed their spacecraft on the far end of a Texas ranch. There, they spotted a shiny red truck, the first they had ever seen. Inside the cab was a skateboard. There were no signs of life.

    "How do you think this wonder came about?" asked Professor Tskawizt.

    "There must have been an explosion," answered Professor Gintkizini.

    "In my educated opinion," launched Professor Tskawizt, "billions of years ago this planet was more favorable to manufacturing. Surrounding the planet was an ooze rich with metals, plastics, rubber, gasoline, and pieces of paint. Eons rolled by and the inevitable happened—this pre-truck was formed by random chance," he said, pointing to the skateboard. "Through ages of evolution a motor was assembled, a steering wheel appeared, and the wheels, through multiple mutations, grew larger and developed rubber treading through the process of random selection. The pieces of red paint somehow were attracted to the outer surface while white paint particles randomly covered the dials and speedometer. Tiny pieces of black paint coincidentally adhered to the white to form all the numbers and letters. During the ice age, a frozen chunk of gasoline was transported to its place under the hood by natural forces and a metal tank gradually formed around it. Once the ice melted, the tank was full of gasoline."

As he put the key in the ignition and turned it, he found that the vehicle would transport them. What a lucky set of coincidences.

2. From your list of illogical presuppositions, check those that would also apply to the theory that everything in the universe evolved without an intelligent designer.

WORDS TO LIVE BY

When I consider your heavens,
 the work of your fingers,
the moon and the stars,
 which you have set in place,
what is man that you are mindful of him?
 —Psalm 8:3–4

How many are your works, O Lord!
 In wisdom you made them all;
 the earth is full of your creatures.
 —Psalm 104:24

I am the Lord,
who has made all things,
who alone stretched out the heavens,
who spread out the earth by myself.
 —Isaiah 44:24

4

HOPE IS SPELLED
G-O-D

Every theory of how the universe came into existence comes back to the same questions. Who or what started it all? What is the origin of that someone or something?

Carl Sagan, a leading spokesperson for the evolutionary theory, stated, "Human beings (and all the other species) have slowly evolved by natural processes from a succession of more ancient beings with no divine intervention along the way."[1]

But where did these more ancient beings come from? If they arose from slime, by merely physical and chemical forces, how did the slime get there? If life evolved from nonliving molecules, who or what created the molecules? If genetic mutations caused all the changes that account for the great variety of living things, where did the original genes come from?

Some experts claim that the universe is expanding and running down. If that claim is interpreted as the universe's having an extremely hot and compact beginning that resulted in a "big bang," who was behind the "big bang"? (It's true that only explosions cause things to expand and run out of energy, but every explosion that is not carefully planned and controlled is destructive and extremely unlikely to produce order. And no one seriously claims that an explosion started life.)

Together with Stephen Hawking, the world famous physicist from Cambridge, we can ask, "How or why were the laws and the initial state of the universe chosen?"[2]

It's hard to believe that chance plus time came up with the forces that keep everything in the universe from falling apart. Gravitational forces hold galaxies, stars, and planetary systems together. They also enable planets to hold on to their atmospheres and moons.

Electromagnetic forces hold molecules together as well as the groups of molecules that form solids and liquids. The centers of atoms are held together by nuclear force, which is the most powerful natural force.[3] The energy inside the atom is so great that if the entire U.S. ran on nuclear power, it would require only forty-three grams or one-and-a-half ounces of enriched uranium per person per year for fuel.[4]

It takes a blind faith to accept without evidence or reason that these incredible forces just happened by chance.

The bright-eyed six-year-old and the cynical college professor often ask the same question: "Who created God?" People scoff at the answer, "God has always existed." But those who ridicule that answer passionately believe things like "matter has always existed" or "there are an infinite number of universes" or "life came from outer space." Yet few ask who or what created matter and universes in the first place.

Because everything boils down to either "God has always existed" or "matter has always existed," it's wise to ask, Which makes more sense?

- God created everything.
- Impersonal matter, over time and by chance, turned into everything.

A careful observer realizes that chance doesn't produce complicated things. No one would believe that the current best-selling mystery is an authorless book produced by monkeys randomly typing letters on sheets of paper. Thus, the sheer complexity of living things requires a designer.

Not only are organisms extraordinarily complicated, each also comes with special equipment for surviving in the environment in which it is placed. "Perhaps the biggest problem for evolutionists is 'the marvelous fit of organisms to their environment.'… Evolutionists from Darwin to Lewontin and Gould admit that 'perfection of structure' has always been 'the chief evidence of a Supreme Designer.'"[5] A trial and error system that depends upon chance doesn't come up with that kind of perfection!

DOES IT MATTER?

Sitting alone in his room, Alex reflected on Saturday night's rave party. It was now Monday and he felt lonely, miserable, and empty. He liked the way the ecstasy made him feel, but he realized that he was becoming psychologically addicted. He wanted to be high all the time, and a TV special on the dangers of ecstasy made him fearful.

But what else was there to live for? "Life is what you make it" was his motto. "We're accidents of evolution," he'd concluded. "There is no God and no life after death. All you have is now—make the most of it."

Alex's dad lived to make money and to accumulate things, but it didn't make him happy. When Alex was little, he liked being the smartest kid in class, but in high school, nerds were decidedly uncool. He thought falling in love was the answer—until Crystal met Colin and abruptly broke up with Alex.

He just couldn't find anything worth living for.

VITAL INFORMATION

Since nothing changes without some external influence and everything that happens has a cause, it is illogical to believe that the universe just accidentally appeared from nothing.

If there exists an uncreated and eternal God—who operates in another dimension and is made out of different stuff than we are—there are real answers to the questions, "How did the universe get here?" and "How can I find meaning in life?"

There's a reason why nothing on this planet ultimately fulfills us.

We were made for another world—one without sickness, death, hate, and unhappiness. God has created us with eternity in our hearts—what Pascal labeled, a "god-shaped vacuum."

When dreams fade, or plans fall through, or friends move, we realize, "If this life is all there is, it's not worth living." But there is more—a lot more.

You can become intimately acquainted with the one Person who will never cease to exist and will always give meaning to your life. We weren't designed to find our own way in a big bad world, or to define what is worthwhile and what is not worthwhile, to live without purpose and to die without hope. We were created to be protected, guided, and forgiven by an eternal God who wants us to spend forever with Him in heaven.

IF ALEX DECIDES TO KEEP LOOKING FOR HOPE, THIS COULD BE HIS EXPERIENCE . . .

Alex sat in sixth-hour biology class, and what he was hearing was too depressing to be boring. "Science has proven," declared Mr. Kennedy, "that we all evolved from lower life forms, and like so many of them, Homo sapiens will someday be extinct. I know that some people need to believe the myths from Genesis but, personally, I can live with the facts."

Dan raised his hand. "Is there scientific evidence that substantiates the claim that life arose from nonlife, and then went through the changes represented on the evolutionary ladder?"

"Within your lifetime," responded Mr. Kennedy, "I'm convinced that scientists will create life in a test tube."

"If they succeeded," responded Dan respectfully, "wouldn't that be creating life by intelligent design?"

"Are you one of those Bible-believing Christians?" asked Mr. Kennedy, trying to hide his disdain.

"Yes, I am," Dan replied without flinching. "But that doesn't mean I'm not interested in getting correct information."

Alex and everyone else listened intently. Mr. Kennedy was an insecure and unpopular teacher. Dan was the new kid at Central High, and the word was, Dan was a brain. An article in the town newspaper identified him as the smartest quarterback that ever played for Central.

"'Oxygen destroys the chemical building blocks of life both on land and under water,'" Dan explained, "so in our atmosphere, which contains substantial amounts of oxygen, it would have been pretty difficult for life to have had a causeless beginning. If an atmosphere without oxygen once existed, it couldn't have had an ozone layer. So radiation would have destroyed the DNA and RNA bonds for the protein chains necessary for life.[6] I don't believe scientists will ever make life in a laboratory. But if they did, it still wouldn't prove that life could have spontaneously erupted on earth without an intelligent Designer."

"This is biology, not a religion class, Daniel," Mr. Kennedy shot back.

"I understand." Dan remained unruffled. "All my information comes from scientists with Ph.D.'s. I'll bring you the sources tomorrow."

Mr. Kennedy flushed, as some of the students broke out into applause. A couple of students jeered, "Hey, Mr. Kennedy, what about that?" and "Yeah, is what Dan says true?"

Dan raised his voice enough to be heard above the noise. "I'm a Christian," he said simply, and waited for quiet. "The Bible teaches us to respect authority. Mr. Kennedy is our teacher, and we should pay attention in his class."

This flustered Mr. Kennedy even more. He appeared awkward as he killed time until the bell rang and school was dismissed for the day. Alex was one of the students who clustered around Dan. "I'll be in the lunchroom," Dan said softly. "I'd be glad to answer any questions there."

Liz and Alex were the only ones who followed. The three of them talked for a couple of minutes about life from a test tube. Then Dan cleared his throat. "The reason I think it's important to tell the truth about God's creating the universe is because it gives us all hope. Last year, my mother died of a heart attack. After that my life totally fell apart."

Alex and Liz paid close attention.

"My mother was a university professor, and she divorced my father when I was six. She'd always said, 'Even if God does exist, I don't need

Him.' But God used an amazing bunch of circumstances to make me see that He's always existed . . . and that He made the universe . . . and that He'd always be there for me."

Dan sat relaxed and confident as he continued. "My dad remarried and started a new family, and after my mom died I moved in with them. But Dad's new wife didn't want me around. Without God I'd have never survived the rejection of my stepmother. I moved here to live with my grandmother. I'd only met her a few times, but with God's help we're getting to know each other.

"Without hope," Dan said, leaning toward Alex and Liz, "I would've seriously considered suicide."

Dan smiled then and looked at his watch. "I'd be glad to talk with you all later," he said. "But I better not be late for football practice."

Slowly Alex walked out of the school building into a gorgeous fall afternoon. The red and gold leaves on the surrounding hills glowed in the sunlight, reflecting in the lake. *There must be hope,* he thought. *Somebody pretty smart must have made all this stuff. If God's a genius, maybe He can even understand me.*

Realizing that someone very intelligent is behind all the wonders of the world and deciding to get to know Him can bring hope and purpose to your life as well. Where there's life—which points toward the Creator of all things—there most definitely is hope. And hope is spelled G-O-D.

ACTION STEPS FOR CHECKING OUT GOD'S EXISTENCE

1. Carefully observe everything around you in nature and ask, "How do the things God made reveal His character?"
2. Read Psalms 96–100; 102:12–27; 103. Write down everything you learn about God.
3. Read the gospels written by Mark and John, remembering that Jesus was God in human flesh. List all the characteristics of God that are found in Jesus.
4. Read about Job's encounter with God in Job 38:1–42:6.

WORDS TO LIVE BY

The eternal God is your refuge,
and underneath are the everlasting arms.
—Deuteronomy 33:27

Now to the King eternal, immortal, invisible, the only God,
be honor and glory for ever and ever.
—1 Timothy 1:17

THIS WAY OUT

The human brain is "the most complex and orderly arrangement of matter in the universe."[1] So states scientist and author Isaac Asimov. The brain weighs about three pounds and contains over 10 billion neurons, or brain cells, each of which has contact with 10 thousand other neurons, requiring a total of 100 trillion neurological interconnections. If all the neurons and threadlike connections of the brain were laid end to end, they would circle the equator four times.[2]

Yet the human brain is 80 percent water—more watery than our blood—so we all have water on the brain! The brain is immune to pain—headaches come not from the organ itself but from the nerves and muscles lining it.[3]

If you think a library contains a lot of information, consider that the brain can hold the information content of twenty-five million books, which would fill a bookshelf five hundred miles long.[4] It's been estimated that by the time a person turns thirty, he or she will have a mental videotape library of about three trillion visualized experiences.[5]

We still don't know, however, precisely what thinking is—or what distinguishes the mind from the brain. That distinction has not yet been shown by studying brain matter.[6] We do know, however, that the human mind is more than the physical stuff inside a person's skull. The brain of a person who just got shot in the heart contains the same amount of physical matter as it did two minutes before, yet it cannot think.

Language learning is another remarkable function of the brain. "The brain is capable of thinking at a rate of 800 words per minute"[7] in one of the world's more than five thousand languages.[8] The average person spends ten to twelve years of his or her life talking.[9] Language, in fact, sets humans apart from animals. Noam Chomsky, a famous linguist, maintains that "the language capacity reveals special design properties that are entirely lacking in the communication systems of other species."[10]

It's true that trained apes and chimpanzees can recognize quite a number of words or visual gestures. Nevertheless, apes are universally incapable of entering the realm of abstract thought.[11] They can not, for example, ask questions, form structured sentences, refer to the past, or indefinitely expand their vocabulary.[12] Einstein and many others have observed that only an intelligent designer could account for the human ability to assign words, gestures, and written symbols to objects, actions, and ideas.[13]

The amazing capacity of humans to think in words and to reflect on the abstract enables us to know God. We can realize we desperately need the Lord and, because of that, reach out to Him. Consider that no animal decides that life isn't worth living and attempts suicide or begins to pray!

Humans also can make decisions about almost everything—where to go for vacation, how to decorate a room, or whether or not to learn to swim. In contrast, an animal's choices are limited. Monarch butterflies always winter in Mexico, robins build the same kind of nest every time, and if Fido gets thrown into the river, he automatically begins to dog paddle—all by instinct.

You, however, have been given the ability to determine many things for yourself—even your eternal future. The most important decision you can make is to seek to know God.

DOES IT MATTER?

Karalee laid her fashion magazine on the coffee table. The clothes featured wouldn't look good on a girl who was thirty pounds overweight, and focusing her attention upon the super slim models made her even more depressed. The two candy bar wrappers and an empty cola can that sat on the table seemed to accuse her. But food was her only refuge in a world where she never seemed to measure up.

Her D in geometry really angered her father, who assumed she wasn't even trying. But maybe it was easier to take the scolding than to admit that she just couldn't understand math. Her mother compared her to her sister who was slender, smart, and popular.

Karalee didn't know what to do. Everything seemed to be closing in on her, and there seemed to be no way out. Jane, one of her few friends at school, said she prayed about her problems. But Karalee wasn't even sure God existed. Her grandfather always said, "If there's a God, He should at least put a loudspeaker in the sky to advise us that He's really up there."

For Karalee, every day was a contest to see whether or not she could meet everyone's expectations—and every day she lost.

VITAL INFORMATION

Within all humans is a longing for something better than our current experience. That longing was placed there so that we'd search for God. The Lord has put within us, too, intelligence and language skills, enabling us to know enough about Him to have a relationship with Him. In addition, it was God who took the initiative in showing Himself to us.

Hebrews 1:1–3 tells us how God revealed to us who He is: "In the past God spoke… through the prophets"—who wrote down what He said in the Bible. God proclaimed the Ten Commandments from Mount Sinai, for example, and they are recorded in the Scriptures. "But in these last days," Hebrews continues, "he has spoken to us by his Son, … the exact representation of his being."

So you can learn about God by discovering what the Bible says about Him. You can learn to know God personally through His Son Jesus, who—as God in human form—came to earth to show us what God is like.

KARALEE COULD FIND FREEDOM FROM
NOT LIVING UP TO FALSE
EXPECTATIONS IN THIS WAY . . .

It was the Saturday before Easter, and Karalee was home alone. Her sister was out on a date and her parents were attending an important social function. When she flicked on the television, the movie channel was showing a film about the life of Christ. A leper knelt before Jesus, and the hopeless look on the face of the leper caught Karalee's attention. She was also attracted to the compassion and kindness Jesus demonstrated when He reached out to heal the man. Jesus imparted hope—not only to the man but to Karalee as well.

In another scene, a woman knelt by Jesus. Her tears flowed on His feet as He reclined at a banquet table, and the woman wiped Jesus' feet with her hair and poured perfume on them. The others at the banquet disapproved and made snide remarks. But Jesus defended this sinful woman, who was desperate to be loved and accepted by Him. He offered her understanding and forgiveness.

Karalee was impressed that Jesus cared about people who didn't fit society's mold. In the movie, Jesus told a story that touched her heart. It was about a proud and foolish son who made terrible decisions. In spite of this, his father accepted him back again with open arms.

Then Peter denied three times that he knew Jesus, yet the Savior, who was about to be crucified, looked at him across the courtyard with loving eyes.

Karalee couldn't imagine being really loved whenever she blew it big time. In her experience, love had to be earned, and she wasn't very good at earning it. It struck her that everything Jesus said and did communicated unconditional love.

The conversation between Jesus and Philip really interested Karalee. Philip had asked, "Lord, show us the Father and that will be enough for us" (John 14:8). Jesus' answer proved that He was God in human form: "Don't you know me, Philip, even after I have been among you such a long time? Anyone who has seen me has seen the Father" (John 14:9).

Karalee became convinced that Jesus really is God, and that He came to earth to live in a body like everyone else in order to demonstrate to the world God's characteristics, attitudes, and truth. This was a much better idea than placing a loudspeaker in the sky!

As she watched hardened Roman soldiers drive nails into Jesus' hands, she also heard Him pray, "Father, forgive them, for they do not know what they are doing" (Luke 23:34). Even when He was dying, Jesus showed love and hope to the criminal who was on the cross next to Him.

Karalee cried because Jesus' love for her seemed tangible and real. She realized that being overweight, having a hard time in school, and not having a lot of friends wouldn't interfere with Jesus loving and accepting her.

But there was more. Jesus conquered death and gloriously appeared to His disciples again, promising them power from on high before He ascended to heaven.

Karalee saw that Jesus offered the things she needed most:

- love she didn't need to earn
- forgiveness for real sins
- freedom from having to fit society's norms
- an outside source of power to help her live correctly
- hope for the future

If God is like Jesus, and now Karalee was sure that He is, He is knowable and definitely worth getting acquainted with.

Like Karalee, you should consider beginning a relationship with the One who gave you your amazing brain, who gave you the desire to find purpose in life, and who gave you the capacity for giving and receiving love. Wouldn't it be encouraging to get input directly from God—the Mastermind who gave you your ability to use language and the creativity you display? You can have a Friend who will always be there for you—even when no one else understands.

ACTION STEPS FOR GETTING ACQUAINTED WITH JESUS

1. Study the encounters people had with Jesus when He lived on the Earth:
   - a leper (Mark 1:40–42)
   - a bad girl from the streets (John 8:1–11)
   - a Jewish leader who would lose his reputation and maybe his job if he followed Jesus (John 3:1–21)
   - a foreigner who dared to trust Jesus (Luke 7:1–10)
   - some young fishermen who didn't know what to do with their lives (Matthew 4:18–22)
   - a woman who took the initiative in showing her love for Jesus (John 12:1–11)
2. Read famous things Jesus said about:
   - hypocrisy and prayer (Matthew 6:1–14; 7:7–12);
   - love (Matthew 5:43–48);
   - how to recognize a phony (Matthew 7:15–20);
   - Himself (John 5:19–24; 8:31–36; 12:44–50; 14:6–17).
3. Read what those who knew Him best said about Him:
   - John, the apostle who was closest to Him (John 1:1, 14; 1 John 1:1–10)
   - Peter, who lived with Him and the other disciples for three-and-a-half years (1 Peter 2:21–25; 2 Peter 1:16–18)
   - James, a half-brother of Jesus (James 1:1; 2:1)
   - Jude, a half-brother of Jesus (Jude 1, 4, 24, 25)

   Have you seriously thought that anybody you knew well might be God? It's amazing that all these men who knew Jesus closely all believed He was God.
4. Give your life to Jesus.

WORDS TO LIVE BY

In the beginning was the Word, and the Word was with God, and the Word was God. . . . The Word became flesh and made his dwelling among us. We have seen his glory, the glory of the One and Only, who came from the Father, full of grace and truth.

—John 1:1, 14

Now this is eternal life: that they may know you, the only true God, and Jesus Christ, whom you have sent.

—John 17:3

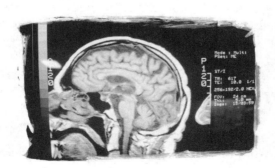

6

SOMEBODY LOVES YOU

A newborn baby has 350 bones. Many of them are soft and pliable, which makes it possible for a normal birth to occur without injury to the baby. These will gradually fuse (grow together) into the 206 bones that are standard for adults.[1]

An adult's bones are so lightweight that they make up only one-fifth of a body's total weight.[2] Yet bones are marvels of flexibility and strength. In addition, some contain "factories" that produce red blood cells to carry oxygen to tissues, platelets that enable blood to clot, and white blood cells capable of fighting infection.[3]

The thighbone, although hollow, is the strongest bone in the body.[4] It's stronger than reinforced concrete and must bear an average of twelve hundred pounds of pressure per square inch with every step. The mid-shaft of the thighbone is able to support a force of six tons before fracturing.[5]

The fifty-two small bones in our feet are, all together, super strong. When a soccer player subjects these bones to a cumulative force of over one-thousand tons for each foot, his or her bones endure the stress and maintain their elasticity. And that's good news for ordinary people who will walk some 65,000 miles during a lifetime—equal to jogging around the earth two and one-half times.[6]

Bones are constructed, then, of tough substances—mineral crystals (mostly calcium and phosphorus), collagen (a gelatinous substance), and cells. But not the *same* crystals, collagen, and cells have done all that work, because the adult skeleton gradually replaces itself about every seven years.[7]

In a small child, 100 percent of the bones are replaced every year. But the child appears the same. Each of the billions of active bone cells, called osteoblasts, has the identical DNA instructions for designing bones that will look the same as the ones replaced, except in the next bigger size.[8]

You can be sure that God keeps track of each cell that is working on something as important as bone replacement. He even monitors things as seemingly inconsequential as the number of hairs on our heads.

Those hairs are, indeed, plentiful. The average adults has 100,000 to 200,000 hairs.[9] As strong as aluminum,[10] a single hair lives about four years before it drops out and is replaced.[11] Within a lifetime, each hair follicle will grow about twenty-six feet of hair, and the entire scalp will produce nearly five hundred miles of hair—one thousand inches of hair each day.[12]

Jesus said something amazing about hair: "Even the very hairs of your head are all numbered. So don't be afraid" (Matt. 10:30–31). When you're in love, every detail about that special person is important to you. God loves you so much that He not only keeps track of the number of hairs on your head, He knows your every thought, follows you wherever you go, and is concerned about your every need.

This constant caring is reflected in the way He made your body; in the beauty of nature, which He created for us to enjoy; in the variety of tastes, colors, and aromas for us to savor; in the unique personalities that He placed within each of us and our friends.

DOES IT MATTER?

Riley was an only child, and his doting parents had always given him everything he wanted. He grew up trying to avoid work and other unpleasant activities. He lived for the moment—his goal in life was to have as much fun as possible. He basically didn't give the future, God, or religion a second thought.

Although he was undisciplined, he was smart enough to do okay in school—until he started hanging out with friends who skipped classes. It wasn't long before he, too, was hooked on ditching school. The class-room felt like a prison. In order to cover his tracks, he became a tal-ented liar.

He started experimenting with drugs and alcohol, until escaping from reality became his reason for living. One day Ned, who looked a lot older than he was, succeeded in buying a case of beer, and four guys, including Riley, celebrated big time. Suddenly, Adrian looked at his watch and panicked. "If I'm not home by three-thirty, my dad will kill me!"

"I'll give you a ride," Riley offered, and the two of them ran for his car. Riley revved the motor and they sped away. He exceeded the speed limit and realized too late that he had missed a stop sign. When he slammed on his brakes, his car skidded on the ice and hit two sixth-grade girls who were crossing the street on their way home from school. Jumping out of the car, Riley and Adrian saw that neither of the girls was getting up. One was bleeding profusely and moaning, while the other lay perfectly still.

VITAL INFORMATION

"If God is love, why do accidents happen?"
"If God cares, why did He let me get addicted to drugs?"
"Why does God allow poverty?"

Many people ask these questions. God chose to give you—and the other six billion people on the planet—a free will. You get to choose between good and evil, but sin always has bad consequences.

What would you think of parents who locked their child in an iron cage so he or she would never total the car, become an alcoholic, con-tract AIDS, or rob a bank? Is that a good way for a loving parent to teach a child how to make wise decisions?

God is the ultimate good and loving parent, and He allows us to make our own choices, to experience the consequences of those choices, to learn from the experience. But all of us, without exception, have used this freedom to make bad choices—to sin. And sin separates us from God. But God loves us and cares about us so much, He provided a way to heal that separation.

As the undeniable evidence of God's great love for each one of us, He allowed Jesus, His only Son, to die for our sins. But Jesus rose again so that His Spirit can live on the inside of any person who is willing to confess sin, to forsake sin, and let Jesus control all areas of life.

When Christ lives in you, it's like having a personal body, soul, and spirit guide—Someone who always loves and cares for you.

IF RILEY HANDLES THE CONSEQUENCES FOR HIS WRONGDOING THOUGHTFULLY, THIS COULD BE THE CONTINUATION OF HIS STORY . . .

Adrian whipped out his cell phone and called 911. Riley just stood there in shock, not knowing what to do. A car stopped, and the lady who got out said she was a nurse. She asked Riley for his scarf and turned it into a tourniquet to stop the bleeding from the girl's leg. As she checked the pulse of the other girl, both the ambulance and the police arrived. Noticing tears in the nurse's eyes, Riley was filled with panic.

Once the two girls were placed in the ambulance, the officers hauled Riley and Adrian off to the police station. Riley's nightmare was just beginning. As he and Adrian waited, they overheard the sergeant answer a phone call—one of the girls had died.

Riley was charged with drunk driving, and until a trial could determine his fate, his license was revoked, and he was placed on a surveillance program.

His life totally changed. The accident was top local news, so everybody knew what had happened. If he skipped school or broke his curfew, he'd be in even more trouble. Confused and scared, Riley operated like a robot who went to classes, studied a little, and watched TV a lot.

Some kids at school stared at him as if he were a criminal. Others didn't know what to say to him. Since he didn't dare skip school, he lost the friends he used to hang out with.

Then one day, Jeremy sat down beside him in the lunchroom. "You must really be hurting," he said. "I've been praying for you."

Riley was shocked that Jeremy, a senior, seemed interested in him. When he was a freshman and Jeremy was a sophomore, they'd been in chess club together, but they hadn't seen much of each other since then.

"God loves you and wants to help you," Jeremy said quietly.

Riley was silent. He didn't dare ask the real question on his mind about why God let his car hit the girls. He couldn't face another reminder of personal responsibility, so he came up with a decoy.

"I don't get it," Riley finally blurted out. "How could a loving God permit old age and suffering? I just visited my grandfather in a nursing home. To tell the truth, that place gives me the creeps."

"If this life were the end, it wouldn't make sense," Jeremy agreed. "But old age reminds everyone that this life won't last forever. That's why we should get right with God, so we can enjoy eternal life in heaven with Him. Sometimes the things that happen to us are unpleasant, but God can use it for good, to bring us closer to Him."

Just then the fire alarm sounded. They had to leave their hot pizza and go out into subfreezing weather without their jackets. There'd been a lot of false alarms lately, and Riley was really upset. Jeremy simply took it all in stride.

As they stood there in the cold, Riley wondered about heaven. His dad considered it a fairy tale, but what if it was real? Riley wanted to make sure he got there.

When the all clear sounded, students filed back into the building, and Riley and Jeremy sat down to cold pizza. Riley hesitated, then sent up another smoke screen. "But how could a loving God allow someone to be born retarded or crippled or with a heart defect?"

"No one really knows why unfortunate things happen to innocent people," Jeremy answered. "But I think it's because God wants the whole family to learn to trust and depend upon Him more. My nine-year-old brother has Down's syndrome, but he's brought a lot of joy to our family. He loves God and even understands what it means to have Jesus in his heart. My whole family is closer to God . . . and we're all closer to each other than we were before he was born."

With that, the bell rang and they hurried off to class. After handing in his math test, Riley started thinking about what Jeremy said about God's love. Riley's definition of showing love was letting someone get his or her own way, or letting a person off the hook. Yet if his parents had been stricter and had insisted that he take more responsibility, he might not be in this current mess.

Jeremy says that God's love means allowing what's best for me in the long run, Riley thought. *If heaven is part of the long run, God might have good reasons for permitting things that we think are unloving.*

Jeremy seemed to have a handle on life and a purpose for living. Knowing God appeared to be the key to his success. Kids teased Jeremy for being part of the "God squad," but that didn't seem to bother him.

When Jeremy won the city chess tournament, he was interviewed on TV, but he didn't take the credit. Instead, he said, "I thank God for giving me the ability to win the tournament." Yet he was a regular guy and fun to be around.

Riley began to entertain the thought that God really *did* love him and intended to use all that had happened for his good. He decided he'd go back to chess club so he'd have an opportunity to ask Jeremy more questions.

Consider this—the God who so carefully rebuilds your bones and counts each hair on your head has a genuine interest in your well-being because He loves you. Isn't it time for you to respond to His love so it becomes a reality in your daily life?

ACTION STEPS TO UNDERSTANDING GOD'S LOVE

1. Remember that God best demonstrates His love by providing us an opportunity for eternal salvation—not by always giving

us what we think we want. To appreciate the full extent of God's love for you, read Luke 22:39–44 and 23:32–39.

2. Since getting us to heaven is the most loving thing God could ever do, reflect on how things like an accident, a financial problem, or a terrorist attack might benefit us spiritually.

3. Someone has said, "Every miracle starts with a problem." Think of ways that an illness, a family problem, a physical handicap, or a demanding teacher might improve your prayer life and cause you to exercise more faith.

4. Answer honestly. When do you seek God most? When things are going well or when there's a big problem?

WORDS TO LIVE BY

But God demonstrates his own love for us in this: While we were still sinners, Christ died for us.

—Romans 5:8

The Lord disciplines those he loves.

—Hebrews 12:6

This is love: not that we loved God, but that he loved us and sent his Son as an atoning sacrifice for our sins.

—1 John 4:10

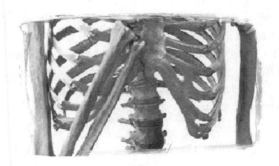

7

WHO'S IN CHARGE HERE?

In outer space, the biggest objects aren't the heaviest. The largest stars don't necessarily contain the greatest amount of matter.[1]

Earth's moon weighs 81 billion billion tons,[2] and the moon is a lightweight by space standards. A single cubic inch of the Star LP327-186, a white dwarf smaller than the state of Texas, weighs several tons.[3]

Neutron stars are even more dense. A neutron star only five miles wide could weigh twice as much as our sun.[4] One cubic centimeter (the size of a finger tip) of a neutron star weighs about the same as 150 million medium-size cars.[5] Or to put it another way, a paper clip made of neutron star material would outweigh Mount Everest![6]

Although some stars are even smaller than Earth's moon, the largest ones have diameters of nearly a billion miles.[7] The red super-giant star Betelgeuse in Orion has a radius almost four times the distance from the sun to the Earth. Betelgeuse is so big that Mercury, Venus, Earth, and Mars could line up along its 720 million-mile diameter, and still maintain their current orbits within Betelgeuse.[8]

Besides trillions of stars, very few of which have moons and planets, space is full of comets—about 300 billion in our solar system alone. Many repeatedly pass within sight, yet they never collide with Earth.[9] Haley's Comet comes back every seventy-six years—it passed near the Earth in 1910 and 1986.[10]

The scientific names for "space rocks" are meteoroids and aster-oids. Some meteoroids are rocks that used to be mixed with the ice in a comet's nucleus. Meteoroids usually burn up in the Earth's atmo-sphere, but not always.[11] A meteorite is the part that doesn't burn up and actually reaches the Earth.

The largest meteorite fall in recorded history occurred in China on March 8, 1976. One hundred stones were found, many weighing over two hundred pounds. The largest, 3,902 pounds, landed in Chincheu.[12]

On June 30, 1908, the most famous meteorite fell to Earth. It rocked northern Siberia with a force two thousand times greater than the atomic bomb that was dropped on Hiroshima. The shock of the im-pact was felt fifty miles away, and its descent could be seen in daylight for hundreds of miles.[13] Witnesses reported a blinding light and thun-derous sounds that were audible up to five hundred miles away. As it burned itself up, the meteorite destroyed everything within a diam-eter of more than twenty miles.[14] It's believed that all that commotion was caused by a weak, stony meteorite that was only about thirty-three yards across![15] The largest meteorite on Earth crashed into West Africa in 1920, and weighed in at sixty-six tons.[16]

The craters on the moon and on Mercury reveal that they have experienced more serious damage. We can be thankful that the Earth's atmosphere protects our planet. Jupiter, which is so big that more than one thousand Earths could be placed inside it, acts as a shield for Earth.[17] If Jupiter were not so strategically placed, comets would strike Earth a thousand times more frequently than they do.[18]

And those strikes would take place at space speeds. The Earth trav-els 66,600 miles per hour[19] in its 585 million-mile orbit around the sun.[20] That's over 1.5 million miles a day. If Earth ever stopped revolv-ing it would burst into flames.[21] Our solar system, traveling at 492,000 miles per hour, would take about 230 million years to make a com-plete trip around the center of the Milky Way Galaxy.[22]

So considering the enormous weights and incredible speeds of space objects, and that the Earth weighs only 6,600 billion billion tons,[23] we can be thankful for the gravitational forces that keep such space heavy-weights in place.

But have you ever wondered *who* keeps all the immense, super-heavy, and speeding objects in outer space from crashing into us? It should be obvious that a God who never changes and never goes out of existence set up the physical laws that keep the universe functioning. And He protects us from a too-close encounter with something in outer space that could wipe us out.

Do you think the person who flippantly declares "I am god," or the guru who teaches that humans are to discover the "god within" ever thinks of changing places with the One who put the laws of gravity in effect? Since Creation, these laws have kept the heavenly bodies traveling at just the right speeds in their orbits.

Considering all the objects that travel through space, it's truly amazing that the Earth hasn't been destroyed by a collision with one of them. Just look into the heavens. What you see is only a small part of *one* galaxy in the universe that God created. Clearly, God is made of different stuff from us. That He is above His creation and possesses an intelligence and power that are uniquely His shouldn't be that hard to figure out.

DOES IT MATTER?

Lisa stared at her open history book. Hitler's rise to power was the last thing on her mind, although flunking tomorrow's test could mean an F on her report card.

She hadn't slept well the night before. Besides, she had a terrible head cold that made her miserable. Lisa was diabetic, and stressful situations like these always raised her blood sugar and tempted her to overeat. But if she indulged herself, the state of her health would become even worse, possibly life threatening. When Lisa's grandmother died eighteen months ago, Lisa had ended up in the hospital.

Her present tailspin started last Saturday morning when Jonathan, her steady boyfriend, called. "Lisa . . . I'm sorry about the concert tonight. But . . . we're just not getting along. I've decided to take Marina instead." Before she could even say a word, he hung up. She immediately called her friend Rita and told her what had happened.

Lisa's whole world had revolved around Jonathan, and she'd never sensed that anything was wrong. She tried to think positively and create a new reality, like she'd been taught to do in her meditation class. She reminded herself that she was god and that she only had to realize her full potential.

But Rita's words kept coming back to her. "A god should be able to cure diabetes and make Jonathan love you again. Someone's just selling you a bill of goods."

VITAL INFORMATION

You're not God—or even a part of God. Instead, you were created by the only true God, and He has attributes you do not possess: He never makes a mistake, He has all power, and He knows everything there is to know.

Can you imagine a construction company coming up with galaxies of such immense stars and keeping them all in space without using any cement or steel beams? Could this feat have been pulled off by some blob of energy called a "gestalt"?

If "god is everything and everything is god," then "god" created himself, which makes him simply a created thing. Created things—like stars or animals—will eventually collapse or die. The Bible teaches, though, that the God who made everything is outside of His creation and different from it. He will never die or go out of existence. He cares about you and can be totally trusted.

IF LISA WHOLEHEARTEDLY LOOKS FOR TRUTH AND REALLY TRIES TO FIND GOD, THE CONTINUATION OF HER SEARCH MIGHT READ LIKE THIS . . .

Lisa did flunk the history test—even though she performed all her think-positive rituals before going to school that day. All week, she kept meeting Jonathan and Marina in the halls. They were always holding hands and obviously very much taken with each other.

Repeating "I am god" seemed totally hollow and ridiculous. Nothing she could do would create the new reality of Jonathan returning to her.

She skipped her meditation class because she didn't want to hear that "the visible world has no importance whatsoever, because only the invisible is real." Well, Jonathan and Marina were real—Lisa *saw* them every day, and the heartache they gave her wasn't some figment of her imagination. Her rising blood sugar numbers weren't some fantasy that right thinking could eradicate.

When Lisa went for her monthly checkup, the alarmed doctor put her in the hospital, where her mother came to visit her at noontime. "Pull yourself together, honey," she advised. "No man is worth getting sick over. Believe me, I know. I'm sorry . . . but I have to get back to work. I'll be back to visit you this evening, though."

Her mother's words were less than comforting. *It's just not fair,* Lisa thought. *Other girls can eat hot fudge sundaes or candy bars or popcorn with extra butter when they feel down. But if I stray from my strict diet— even a little—I have serious health problems. That's probably why Jonathan got tired of me. And maybe no man will ever love me again.* She began to cry.

Her pity party lasted so long she didn't even notice that it had been snowing hard for some time. As she looked out the window, she saw the ugly gray of the city being blanketed with a soft and silent cover of white. The wonder of it made her forget for a few minutes about her tears. She gazed over the unbroken, pure white.

That night, she saw the full moon turn the snow into silvery majesty. And when the sun came out the next day, the snow sparkled like millions of diamonds. Lisa felt small and insignificant in the presence of such beauty and wonder. She decided that Rita was right. God was superior to all the things He had made—and she had been created by this awesome God.

Her thoughts were interrupted when a nurse entered the room. She was leading a girl who had ugly scars on her face. As the nurse guided the girl to the other bed in the room, Lisa realized that the girl was blind. After the nurse showed the girl where everything was, she told her that a doctor would come to explain the operation in more detail.

When the nurse left, the girl smiled and said, "I guess we should get acquainted. My name's Rebekah."

"I'm Lisa—glad to meet you."

"I'm here for another operation," Rebekah said. "The operations to restore my sight were unsuccessful, but this one will take away my scars . . . and make me look like other people."

Lisa hesitated, looking at Rebekah. "Do you mind if I ask—"

"What happened to me?"

Lisa mumbled something.

"It's okay. Everybody asks. There was an explosion in chem lab."

"How did it happen?" asked Lisa.

"Two guys were mad at the teacher and changed the labels on his bottles," Rebekah said. "My lab partner and I were the first to try the experiment using the wrong ingredients, and everything blew up in my face."

"You must be furious!" Lisa exclaimed. "Are your parents suing?"

"Actually, I've forgiven Patrick and Cameron," said Rebekah. "Their parents have been good about helping with expenses. I've just gotten a trained guide dog. His name is Duke and, with him, I can go anywhere."

Rebekah smiled, and she spoke in a matter-of-fact way, seeming to hold no bitterness.

"How can you be so calm and forgiving?" Lisa asked. "I'd want to see someone pay, big time!"

"It's my faith," Rebekah stated simply. "I believe that God has charge of absolutely everything. This life isn't all there is. I might spend the rest of my life here as a blind person, but in heaven I'll have a new body and new eyes, and the things I'll see in heaven are more exciting than anything I'll miss here."

Lisa began to realize that pretending she was god and attempting to create her own reality would never give her what Rebekah had.

Whenever you're tempted to follow a philosophy that teaches that you are god, ask yourself if you're ready to keep Earth from colliding with other space objects, and to keep the moon in its orbit.

Reflect a little more. Why miss out on praying for wisdom to a God who is smarter than you are, receiving protection from a God who is all-powerful, and obeying a God whose good plans for you span time and eternity?

ACTION STEPS FOR CELEBRATING A GOD WHO IS ABOVE ALL HE HAS MADE

1. List all the disadvantages of believing that you are God.
2. What things can God do that are beyond your reach?
3. What would you miss out on if you grew up believing that you were God? (Alexander the Great was taught that he was a god. Although he was very successful at first, he came to a point when his army refused to follow him further. He cried because there were no more worlds he could conquer, and at thirty-three years of age, he died of a fever.)
4. Why is it logical to believe that God is above and outside of His creation?

WORDS TO LIVE BY

> In the beginning you laid the foundations of the earth,
>   and the heavens are the work of your hands.
> They will perish, but you remain;
>   they will all wear out like a garment.
> Like clothing you will change them
>   and they will be discarded.
> But you remain the same,
>   and your years will never end.
>
> —Psalm 102:25–27

Do not be quick with your mouth,
  do not be hasty in your heart
  to utter anything before God.
God is in heaven
  and you are on earth,
  so let your words be few.

—Ecclesiastes 5:2

8

RUNNING GOD'S
STOP SIGN

There are twenty-eight types of purebred cats[1] and more than three hundred kinds of purebred dogs.[2] Then, through random crossbreeding, there are, of course, an infinite variety of both cats and dogs. But it's impossible to crossbreed between species. There is not, in other words, a single "catadog."

Programmed into the DNA of every species of every living thing is a genetic code that defines its characteristics.[3] People have tried unsuccessfully to produce new animals that are then capable of reproduction. It's possible to cross a donkey with a horse and come up with a mule. Because all male mules are sterile, however, the few babies that are born to female mules are half-breeds.[4] "Selective breeding of animals is a process guided by intelligence, and it produces only variations within the species."[5]

There's a big difference, then, between the modifications represented in breeding a toy terrier and those portrayed when a dinosaur hypothetically sprouts wings and flies off. The first is an example of an observable change that can occur because the DNA programming in dogs allows for a lot of variation. But all dogs bark, walk on all fours, and have wet noses. None can talk, do math homework, or live in the ocean. The DNA programming of reptiles, however, doesn't equip them for flight.

There are limits, then, to documented changes—sometimes called microevolution—within an animal group. For instance,

- "Natural selection can move the species only a limited distance from the species norm."[6] It's impossible, for example, to breed a dog much smaller than a teacup poodle.[7]
- The more an animal differs from the species norm, the lower its chance of survival.[8] That's why the common mutt needs little attention while the tiny purebred requires a lot of special care.
- "The production of a new animal species in nature has yet to be documented."[9] If human-designed breeding were to stop and animals such as dogs, horses, or pigeons were allowed to freely mate, this "random selection" would not result in a new species that was part dog and part horse. Rather the result would be all species quickly reverting to the characteristics of their wild ancestors.[10]
- Because of environmental changes, the prevalent color of peppered moths can change, but they won't learn to sing like birds or turn into dragons.[11]
- If a new predator is introduced, the average size of guppies (bright-colored fish often used in goldfish bowls) can increase in sixty generations, but they don't turn into philosophers. Neither do algae grow up to become octopuses.[12]

The genetic programming that God created in living things gives each species certain characteristics. Those characteristics set the boundaries for environments within which each species can be healthiest and happiest. Within those limits, however, God created enough genetic variety so that some species have the potential for change in order to survive in or adapt to a variety of environments.

God created limits for humans too. But humans, unlike animals, get to make significant behavioral choices. That's because the boundaries that God set for us are not straightjackets to keep us from achieving or from enjoying life. Exactly the opposite is true.

God gives us the liberty to express our personalities, creativity, and talents in ways that don't violate His holiness. Thus, He put within us the ability to adjust to new situations, to overcome obstacles, and to enjoy challenges. The purpose of His guidelines is to keep us from self-destruction, so deciding to defy the rules set up by our Creator is unwise. The further we stray from God's standards and command-ments, the greater the risk of chaos, pain, and heartbreak.

Ecclesiastes 12:1 is excellent advice for your future happiness: "Re-member your Creator in the days of your youth." Realizing that God made you and that He knows what will give you fulfillment can keep you from making many poor choices.

DOES IT MATTER?

Julie stared at the big red letters on her alarm clock. It was 2:07 A.M., and she was still awake. Her fast-lane life usually kept her too busy to think. But a gnawing fear kept her mind in turmoil. For two weeks she'd been fighting nausea—every morning. When she came home from school yesterday, her mother was cooking sauerkraut, and the smell caused her to throw up before she could reach the bathroom.

She had faked her way through her mother's questions. But one big fear prevented her from sleeping. Could she be pregnant? She'd been having sex with her boyfriend Damian for over five months. But they'd planned everything, and she'd faithfully taken her birth control pills.

When sleep came at last, Julie's dreams replayed all the rebellion and defiance that had lead to this moment. She'd detested her parents for their moral absolutes and old fashioned rules, questioned the jus-tice of God, and made fun of the Bible. She'd skipped youth meetings and lied about where she'd been. She'd experimented with drugs and alcohol. She'd been sneaking out with Damian, and finally staged a full-scale tantrum that made her mom feel so guilty that her parents finally gave her permission to date him.

In Julie's nightmare, her mom's warning flashed in neon lights in Times Square: "One sexual mistake can change your life forever."

The next day was Saturday. She manufactured an excuse to leave the house and went to the crisis pregnancy center to be tested. It was positive. Panicking, she called Damian on a pay phone.

His words were chilling: "Have an abortion, or it's your problem and you're on your own." He slammed down the phone.

Julie just stood there, too stunned to react, too devastated to cry.

VITAL INFORMATION

You should fear sin more than anything else in the world. Sin—unless it's confessed and rejected—can steal your happiness, complicate your life, ruin your relationships, and disrupt your communication with God. The Devil, though, can dupe people into rejecting Christ and missing out on heaven, all so that they cling to sinful behavior. The good news is that God not only forgives sin but also supplies the power to overcome it—if you're ready to admit your wrongdoing and follow the prescription Jesus gives for your cure.

IF JULIE DECIDES TO LET GOD RUN HER LIFE FROM NOW ON, THIS COULD BE THE CONTINUATION OF HER STORY . . .

Julie didn't know what to do next. Returning to the compassionate lady at the crisis pregnancy center seemed like her best option.

"Julie," Karen greeted her warmly. "I'm so glad you've come back. Let's go into my office so we can talk."

Karen seated Julie at a small table and took the chair across from her.

"I'd like to begin," Karen spoke easily, "by telling you my story. I got pregnant in high school, and when my boyfriend broke up with me, I had an abortion. I thought it would solve the problem, but it didn't. I felt guilty and dirty. Every time I saw a baby, I felt like crying. I had nightmares and became depressed, but I never told anyone what had happened."

Karen leaned forward and crossed her arms on the table. "In college I dated the captain of the football team. He said he wanted to marry me, and we began having sex. When I got pregnant, he took me to an abortion clinic. I thought that with a man by my side it would be easier . . . but it wasn't. I became depressed again and lost another boyfriend.

"Then I got my dream job and fell in love with my boss. He never told me he was married—until I was pregnant. This time I kept my baby—a beautiful little girl. Before she was born, a friend told me that I could be forgiven and that Jesus could give me new life. I surrendered to His love and, even though being a single mom is difficult, I now have Jesus by my side."

Julie decided to tell Karen everything. She'd been terribly rebellious, her boyfriend had just ditched her, her father was laid off, her little sister had autism, and her grandmother had recently been diagnosed with Alzheimer's disease, which resulted in her living with them. "And I'm going to add to the family's problems," Julie sobbed. "What can I do?"

They talked for a long time, and finally Karen asked Julie if she was ready to totally surrender her life to God. She was, and they prayed together.

Next Karen told her about all the options available. She said they had a list of families who took in pregnant girls, as well as names of approved Christian couples who wanted to adopt babies. Julie decided not to have an abortion.

She still had to face all the terrible consequences of sin—telling her parents, not being able to compete in tennis matches, ending her senior year by dealing with morning sickness, enduring the stares and whispers of others. But Julie felt the love and deep companionship of Jesus.

After a lot of praying, she decided to graduate and then go to live with a family selected by the crisis pregnancy center. She'd stay there until the baby was born and adopted by a Christian couple. She knew she wasn't ready to be a mother and just couldn't add to the family stress.

Parting with her baby boy was harder than she thought it would be, but she had the satisfaction of having given him life and a wonderful

Christian home. More and more she discovered joy and peace in Jesus. No longer did she ride the roller coaster of emotions that were dictated by circumstances. She was sensing the peace that obedience to the Lord brings.

She had experienced the disillusionment of straying from God's boundaries, yet now she was receiving His unconditional forgiveness. She experienced, too, the abundant resources He gives to those living within His will and who trust Him when they face tough times.

Every living thing is meant to conform to the plan its Creator originally had in mind. Animals have no choice but to live within the boundaries of their DNA-programmed capabilities. Crows can't live under water and crocodiles can't climb trees.

Humans, too, usually accept their physical limitations. But they sometimes feel they can defy the moral boundaries that God has put in place—without having to face negative consequences. That simply isn't true. If you, like Julie, have been deceived, it's not too late to align yourself with God's wise principles for better living.

ACTION STEPS FOR RECOVERING AFTER BLOWING IT BIG TIME

1. Take full responsibility for your wrong behavior.
2. Honestly admit everything to God, repenting of your sin and accepting His forgiveness.
3. Receive the love and acceptance of God.
4. Take all of God's commands seriously, relying on the Holy Spirit for the power to obey.
5. When the Devil reminds you of your past, remind him of his future!

WORDS TO LIVE BY

Blessed is he
   whose transgressions are forgiven,
   whose sins are covered.
Blessed is the man
   whose sin the LORD does not count against him
   and in whose spirit is no deceit.

—Psalm 32:1–2

Therefore, if anyone is in Christ, he is a new creation; the old has gone, the new has come!

—2 Corinthians 5:17

LOOKING AT THE BIG PICTURE

The sun's infrared, ultraviolet, and visible light are absolutely necessary for life. (We usually refer to infrared light as heat.) The plants that we eat need light for photosynthesis—the process necessary for plant growth—and photosynthesis emits oxygen—a gas we're all addicted to.

Without light, our eyes couldn't function. We are able to see not only because of natural light from the sun, but because the sunlight that came to Earth years ago enables us to see by artificial light. That sunlight produced plants, which became compressed and formed coal, natural gas, and oil. Those fuels are used today to produce heat, air conditioning, and electricity for our homes.[1]

Clearly, the sun is crucial for life. But because the sun is so huge and so hot, if it were not placed at a suitable distance from us, life could not exist on Earth. The sun's immense size is almost beyond imagination—109 times wider than our Earth, with a volume 1,300,000 times that of the Earth.[2] The sun is so big, in fact, over one million Earths could fit inside it.[3] The temperature on the sun's bright outer layer (which we see from Earth) is eleven thousand degrees Fahrenheit. But that pales in comparison to its core temperature of twenty-seven million degrees Fahrenheit.[4] Temperatures that high would incinerate us if Earth were significantly closer to the sun. But if Earth were positioned too far from the sun, we'd freeze to death.

The sun averages, however, a safe distance of 92,980,000 miles from the Earth. The word *average* is used, because the Earth's orbit around the sun is not a true circle. Depending upon the time of year, the Earth's distance from the sun varies by 3.1 million miles.[5] In early January, the sun is 3 million miles closer to the Earth than it is in early July.[6] For this reason, it takes 8 minutes 10.7 seconds for light to reach Earth in early January, and 8 minutes 27.4 seconds in early July.[7]

No matter how near or how far the sun, though, its light travels at the same speed. Sunlight, or any kind of light for that matter, travels at 186,282 miles per second. Light travels slower through water, glass, and other transparent materials because it stops when it encounters atoms and then starts up again. But between atoms, it resumes its normal speed.[8]

And sunlight's speed, like the sun's distance from Earth, gives us evidence of an intelligent Designer. If light traveled faster, the sun and the other stars would be too bright. But if light traveled slower, the sun and stars wouldn't be bright enough to produce the right elements to maintain life.[9]

The unimpeded speed of light, then, is constant. It is not changed by the speed of its source or the speed of the person measuring it. The light coming from a rapidly moving flashlight, for example, travels at the same speed as the light from a stationary flashlight—and that light would come to *you* at the same speed whether you were running or standing still.[10]

In 1905, Einstein explained that light flows in minute packets of energy called photons. Photons are so small that a 100-watt bulb gives off about 200 million trillion photons a second.[11] Every second, about 3,000 trillion photons of light from the sun fall on every pinhead-sized area of Earth.[12] The Earth only intercepts, though, about one-half of one-billionth of the photons emitted from the sun—the correct amount for our needs.[13]

All the qualities of light are constant, and light is certainly one of God's greatest creations. The things in the universe that remain constant give us a hint of what the Bible means when it refers to God as eternal—above and outside of time and space, the one who has always existed and who will never go out of existence.

Because light is constant—penetrating and consuming darkness, but never absorbed by darkness[14]—it can remind us that God has made us with everlasting souls—that death is not the end of you. The Lord invites you to spend a wonderful eternity with Him.

DOES IT MATTER?

Robbie hobbled into the kitchen to find something to drink. Looking down at the cast on his right leg, he winced with pain as he swung on his crutches. He returned to the table and tried to concentrate on studying for his physics test.

But questions kept racing through his mind. Why had he accepted Jack's invitation to go roller skating? Why had two hotshot seventh graders decided to race across the floor when the rink manager wasn't looking? Why hadn't God kept one of those boys from crashing into him? How come his leg got broken just before baseball season? Why did it have to be a compound fracture that required surgery? He had many more questions—but no answers.

When he was a junior, Robbie was considered the top pitcher in the league. His school, North High, was favored to take the city championship, and Robbie had hoped the coming season's rivalry would attract college baseball scouts. Robbie had dreamed about a scout's taking an interest in him and offering him a scholarship.

But now all his plans were shattered. This accident put his entire life on hold, and he wondered if he'd heal enough to handle even his lifeguard job at the pool this summer. And as for baseball, Robbie was too afraid of the doctor's answer to ask, "Will I fully recover and be able to play as well as I did before the accident?"

VITAL INFORMATION

You will live forever—either in the light and never-ending joy of heaven or in the darkness and horror of hell. Jesus, Himself, made this statement when He was discussing the fate of the ungodly: "They will go away to eternal punishment, but the righteous to eternal life" (Matt. 25:46).

Peter tells us more specifics about the wonderful hope for those who have trusted Jesus: "[They have] an inheritance that can never perish, spoil or fade—kept in heaven for you" (1 Peter 1:4). For this reason, you need to keep things in perspective. You're going to live forever, so the slice of life you're experiencing right now is only a tiny part of the big picture—it's like one photon of light compared with all the sunshine ever produced.

IF HE TURNS TO GOD, ROBBIE MIGHT HAVE AN OUTCOME LIKE THIS . . .

It was the last half of the ninth in North High's first away game against a mediocre team. A three-run homer in the seventh had given North High a 9–6 lead. But bases were loaded in the last of the ninth, and Dereck pitched four straight balls! Frustration overwhelmed Robbie. He felt like hobbling out on his crutches and throwing the ball over the plate. The next batter hit a triple and the game was over.

As Robbie slowly made his way to Jim's car, it seemed like a dozen people told him, "If you'd been pitching, we'd have won." That only made Robbie feel more depressed.

Kara was the only one that made a different comment. "Robbie, now that you have more time, why don't you come to our Bible study?" she asked. "We'll stop by your house at six-fifteen on Tuesday night."

Caught by surprise, Robbie heard himself answer, "Okay."

Kara was very active at school and was the president of North High's Bible club. Robbie attended the same church as Kara, and he'd prayed to receive Christ as a child. But he was a chameleon Christian, changing his colors as necessary to fit in at church or at school. He didn't like being seen with the Bible club kids at school because it might affect his popularity. But since the Bible study met at Matt's house, it seemed safe enough.

On Tuesday evening, six kids took their seats around Matt's dining room table, and opened their Bibles and study guides. Robbie prepared to be bored. When it was his turn to read, however, the verse was James 4:14: "You do not even know what will happen tomorrow.

What is your life? You are a mist that appears for a little while and then vanishes."

"If our whole lives are only like a vapor that quickly disappears," commented Carmen, "we're really wasting our time worrying about things that will soon be over."

"We should look at everything with eternity in mind," said Matt. "There's right-now stuff and forever stuff. If I invest my time in winning and discipling others for Christ, my work lasts beyond this life."

Kara added, "It's all too easy to think that the next test or the next game or getting into the right college is the most important thing in the world. I was way too disappointed when I didn't get the scholarship I wanted. I have to stop thinking in terms of what I want right now. Instead, I need to recognize that God has an eternal plan. Maybe my going to community college will give me a better chance to serve Him."

Robbie realized that he'd been living as if this life were all there is. That's why he worshiped popularity and thought that missing one baseball season was the ultimate tragedy. It occurred to him that if he didn't look at things from the perspective of eternity, he'd be bummed out most of the time.

He'd felt that the Lord was unfair in allowing him to break his leg. But now he understood that God was eternal. From God's better vantage point Robbie knew that his time on crutches would enable him to learn a lesson that would help him all his life.

In his heart Robbie told God that he was sorry for being so self-centered and for concentrating on things that, in a hundred years—in maybe just six months—wouldn't matter. He rededicated his life to his Creator. From now on, he'd plug into God's eternal enterprises instead of putting primary importance on things that last for only a short time.

Physical light allows physical sight. But God is our source of spiritual light, and for this reason Jesus said, "I am the light of the world" (John 8:12). He is the one who gives us the ability to see things from an eternal perspective.

Depending totally upon Jesus to do His will in our lives sparks us with energy, fills us with His love, and provides us with security. Like physical light, Jesus—the Light of the World—comforts us. But darkness is depressing. Life without intimacy with God is lived in a twilight zone where darkness keeps closing in. Join Robbie in coming out into God's light.

ACTION STEPS FOR BREAKING FREE FROM "EARTHBOUNDNESS"

1. List all your worries and all your priorities. Cross out those that will not matter a hundred years from now.
2. Ask God to show you which temporal activities indirectly enable you to do things that will count for eternity. List those things. (Example: Studying enables you to learn things that will improve your ability to witness to certain people. It helps you be a good example of a Christian to your teachers and fellow students. It may help you to get a better job, which will enable you to devote more financial resources for Christian work.)
3. What kinds of eternal investments can you make in the people around you? Be specific.
4. Decide to do one thing this week that could make an eternal difference.

WORDS TO LIVE BY

Do not store up for yourselves treasures on earth, where moth and rust destroy, and where thieves break in and steal. But store up for yourselves treasures in heaven, where moth and rust do not destroy, and where thieves do not break in and steal.
—Matthew 6:19–20

Set your minds on things above, not on earthly things. For you died, and your life is now hidden with Christ in God.
—Colossians 3:2–3

10

GETTING IT ALL TOGETHER

The skin is the largest organ in the body. Weighing eight or nine pounds, the skin covers a surface area of over two square yards, every square inch of which serves a purpose.

First, our skin holds us together. Our bodies are 60 percent water, and without our skin keeping all that liquid inside, we'd turn into puddles!

The skin also lets some water out—in the form of sweat. Perspiration is the body's natural cooling system, protecting us from dangerous overheating.[1] So if you're active on a really hot day, it's possible to lose as much as two gallons of water in perspiration.[2] If we didn't sweat, our internal body-temperatures would rise, and an increase of just seven or eight degrees would kill us.[3]

The skin also is the first line of defense against would-be invaders like liquids, bacteria, and yeast. The skin draws from a variety of chemicals, electronegative charges, and groups of defending cells in order to counterattack the invaders. If someone hits you or you crash into something, the effects of the blow are spread across thousands of skin cells. Those cells spring back like a trampoline, absorbing the impact and shielding internal organs.[4]

We feel pain from that impact because our skin comes equipped with nerve receptors, and the most sensitive areas of our bodies have

thousands of them per square inch. The pain these receptors communicate causes us to remove our hand from the hot stove and makes us
hesitant to walk barefoot over sharp pebbles.[5] Most of us probably
take our sense of touch for granted, but life would be very difficult
without it.

"Scientists disagree on exactly how touch works, but those seemingly useless hairs blanketing our bodies act as levers to magnify the
sensation of touch. We can discern one-thousandth of an ounce of
pressure on the tip of a half-inch hair."[6] Our sense of touch enables us
to detect cracks in a smooth surface. A normal hand can, in fact, discern a line etched in glass only 1/2500 of an inch deep.

Our sense of touch also makes life more pleasurable. Think about
how good it feels to receive a hug, snuggle a kitten, or caress a rose
petal. We feel less pleasant objects too, like earth worms. And the ridges
in our skin, which are different for each person, give us the traction
we need for picking up slippery objects like that worm.[7]

In addition to the practical and life preserving functions, the skin
constantly renews itself. Billions of skin cells slough off every day and
are immediately replaced by new ones. Our epidermis (the outer layer
of skin cells) is replaced every couple of weeks, which is why a suntan
fades. Over a lifetime a person will shed forty pounds of dead skin!

As we grow older, though, our skin's composition changes, losing
much of its elasticity, causing lines and wrinkles. It's been estimated
that it takes 200,000 frowns to make a permanent line. So smiling
might enhance our looks more than skin creams do!

God created our skin to have a lot of important functions, but skin
color is apparently not a major consideration. Less than one-hundredth
of 1 percent of our genetic structure is coded for differences in skin
color.[8]

Rather, skin is important because without it, your body, which contains the "real you," wouldn't hold together. And our skin resembles
God's Word—both form a boundary. Just as the "real you" needs a
body that requires skin to form its boundaries, true spirituality—a
genuine relationship with our Creator—can exist only with the boundaries of God's Word.

In the pages of the Bible, God has given us His very own words—the truth about life, death, reality, eternity, love, and God Himself. Still, people often go through a lot of confusion and trouble trying to "find their own truth" in a religion with which they *feel* most comfortable.

Terrorists and others who kill innocent people in the name of God—or Allah—think they have the truth. Some claim that their visions, or those of a prophet or guru, hold the truth. There are those who say that spirit guides just informed them of the truth. What, then, is right?

Maybe you've wished for "spiritual skin" when it comes to a developing relationship with God—something to keep the good stuff in and protect against what is harmful. You'd like that relationship to be based on the real Truth wouldn't you? Look, then, into God's own Word—the Bible.

DOES IT MATTER?

Trent was Mr. Personality Plus. At ease with people, he enjoyed conversation with just about everybody. Popular and well-liked, Trent was usually the center of attention. People laughed at his jokes and listened to his stories. He could talk his way into and out of almost anything.

But his charming personality led him into temptation. He grew accustomed to exaggerating, making his life sound more exciting than it was. In order to win first place in the school magazine drive, he invented a line that strayed far from the facts. And he'd become quite accomplished at lying to get out of trouble.

All this happened so gradually that he hardly realized it. Yet he considered himself a good Christian and was elected president of his youth group.

When Brandee transferred to their school, Trent—and everyone else—took notice. A strikingly beautiful, natural blond, Brandee was friendly, funny, intelligent, musically talented, and athletic. And she didn't hide her interest in Trent. She showed up at his youth group and even gave a testimony.

Trent invited Brandee to the citywide spring banquet for Christian teens. They really hit it off and had a great time. At school, she started eating with Trent and the other Christian kids.

He began to notice, though, some inconsistencies in her statements. She mentioned having been on the ski team as a sophomore. But a week later she told them she'd completed her first two years of high school in Dallas, Texas, a city not known for its snow cover.

Other things nagged at him too. When Trent wanted to meet Brandee's parents, she said that her mother was ill and needed to recuperate quietly at home. And one day she told Trent she was going to eat lunch with Wynona so she could invite her to the youth rally. When Trent passed their table, he overheard Brandee telling an X-rated joke.

Too many things weren't adding up. Could Trent really believe what Brandee told him?

That afternoon, he stopped by Brandee's house when he knew she'd still be at play practice. A little girl about three years old came to the door. She looked exactly like Brandee. "My mommy's at school," she told Trent, "but I'll get my grandma." Trent just stood there, too stunned to move.

VITAL INFORMATION

You can't separate a person from the things that he or she says. Your words are part of you, revealing more about your character than you can ever imagine.

In the same way, God's Word shows what He is really like. He demonstrates that He is faithful by giving lots of specific prophecies in the Bible about people groups, empires, cities, and Jesus Christ—prophecies that have been fulfilled in every detail. This gives us confidence to believe that those prophecies that haven't happened yet will eventually come to pass. God always keeps His Word.

God has given to us in the Bible many descriptions of Himself. It's dangerous to believe the imagination of another person rather than God's own definition of Himself.

IF TRENT DECIDES TO BE SENSITIVE
TO GOD'S LEADING, THE NEXT
CHAPTER OF HIS LIFE MIGHT READ
LIKE THIS . . .

Once Trent recovered from the shock of Brandee's lying, he was furious. How could anyone be so deceitful? He would call her later— when he knew she'd be home—give her a piece of his mind, and avoid her for the rest of the year.

That evening, though, as he went to the phone to call Brandee, it rang. His youth pastor, Jeff, was on the line, asking if he could drop by to discuss an urgent matter. Because the church was close to Trent's house, and Pastor Jeff would be there soon, Trent decided to call Brandee later.

When Pastor Jeff arrived, he suggested they walk across the street to the park. "Trent," Pastor Jeff began, "it's about the report you gave to the congregation at the service a couple of weeks ago—the one on the youth outreach trip to Grand Falls. The service was taped that evening, and I sent a copy to Pastor Bob in Grand Falls. He said that your report was grossly exaggerated. He also checked the facts with the boys from his group who went witnessing with you. He found out that you invented most of the action. Lindsay and Jenny have confirmed what Pastor Bob said."

For once, Trent was speechless. Looking Trent in the eye, Pastor Jeff continued. "Please understand that lying is very serious. We can't expect God to bless us if we become hypocrites, if we try to receive credit by stretching the truth. I'm going to have to remove you as president of the youth group. I need a president I can trust."

To his credit, Trent made no excuses. His memory convicted him of exaggeration and lying: The line he'd used to sell magazines—what he said hadn't been exactly true. His account of taking the wrong ski trail and being lost for an hour—that had turned into a story about a near-death experience. And his fable about helping a homeless man— that convinced his parents not to punish him for breaking curfew.

With tears in his eyes, Trent prayed with Pastor Jeff, asking for God's forgiveness. He promised he'd apologize to the youth group the following Sunday—and he did.

Soon after, instead of angrily accusing Brandee, he enlisted a couple of compassionate Christian girls from school to try to help her. They went with him when he kindly told Brandee about the inconsistencies he'd noticed. The girls assured her that everyone wanted to keep eating lunch with her at school, and wanted her to attend their youth group.

He also confessed his own fudging on the truth, ending with, "I'm also a recovering 'master of deception,' so I can understand how you got off track."

Trent paused and swallowed hard. "Brandee . . . I won't be asking you out. Both of us need to learn how to tell the truth before we become involved in any dating."

If Trent and Brandee had continued a relationship based upon deception, the end would have been a disaster. To be comfortable in his own skin, Trent, or anyone, needs honest peer friendships as well as a relationship with God that is based upon truth—minus hypocrisy.

Jesus said, "I am . . . the truth" (John 14:6)—and truth matters a whole lot. Any supposed friendship with God that is rooted in misinformation or wrong assumptions will end in disillusionment. So it's essential that your concept of God is based on the truth of Scripture. You need to love, worship, and serve a God who is really there. If you believe in a made-up god, your spiritual experience will be as pathetic as a dysfunctional, skinless body.

ACTION STEPS TO LETTING GOD'S TRUTH GUIDE YOUR LIFE

1. Check out God's definition of the following concepts:
   - love (1 Corinthians 13:4–7);
   - sin (1 John 3:4–6, 9–10);
   - forgiveness (1 John 1:7–10);
   - doing the right thing (John 6:28–29; 1 John 5:3);
   - salvation (Romans 3:22–24; 10:9–10).

2. Compare all spiritual experiences with the truth of God's Word.
3. Find out what God says about the end of the world by checking out the following:
   • Matthew 24–25;
   • Revelation 20:11–22:21.
   Don't just swallow anything that you hear.
4. Instead of inventing your own religion, agree with what God says in the Bible.

WORDS TO LIVE BY

> I have hidden your word in my heart
>   that I might not sin against you. . . .
> The unfolding of your words gives light;
>   it gives understanding to the simple.
>   —Psalm 119:11, 130

Man does not live on bread alone, but on every word that comes from the mouth of God.
                                    —Matthew 4:4

Heaven and earth will pass away, but my words will never pass away.
                                    —Matthew 24:35

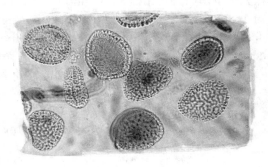

11

GOD'S GOT YOU COVERED

On a clear night you can see a candle flame from thirty miles away.[1]

The human eye is amazing. Here's how it works: Light first encounters the cornea, the transparent outer coating on the eyeball and the primary focusing structure. Light then passes through the iris, which controls the amount of light allowed to enter the eye. The iris is the area surrounding the pupil and gives your eye its coloring.[2] Amazingly, the iris has 266 identifiable DNA-controlled characteristics, more than any other physical body structure. (By comparison, a fingerprint has only about thirty-five measurable traits, so using an iris scanner for identification purposes provides more individual-specific information than fingerprinting.)[3]

Light next moves from the iris to the lens for fine-tuned focusing.

Finally, light reaches the retina, a thin lining in the back of the eye where the image received is converted into electrical signals that can be interpreted by the brain. On the retina are 120 million rods and 7 million cones. Rods give you dim vision, night vision, and peripheral vision, while cones allow you to distinguish millions of shades of color and fine details.

Each eye has one million nerve fibers that electronically connect the photoreceptors in the retina to the visual cortex of the brain (which comprises only 1 percent of the total brain cortex). In this way the image is reconstructed so we "see" it.[4]

John K. Stevens, a biomedical engineer, compares the operation of optical nerve cells to the capabilities of a computer. Because it involves solving hundreds of difficult equations, the Cray supercomputer would need several minutes to do the work that a single nerve cell in the retina completes in ten milliseconds. Because ten million or more nerve cells in the retina interact in complex ways, the Cray supercomputer would need one hundred years to simulate what takes place in your eye many times every second.[5]

Even with almost no light, the eye adjusts, presenting a panorama of black and white and shades of gray, permitting you to "see" in the dark. The eye can also adapt to the sudden intrusion of a bright light. The brightest light the human eye can perceive, in fact, is one billion times brighter than the dimmest.[6]

And you never have to wash your eyes. Tears, which are sterile and contain bacteria-destroying enzymes, do the job for you.[7] By blinking your eyes, you lubricate them. On average, we blink automatically every two to ten seconds—over 400 million times during our lives.[8] If eyelid reflexes are lost, as occurs in persons with Hansen's disease (leprosy), the cornea will dry out, resulting in blindness.[9]

So whenever you watch TV, look at the stars, or read a book, you are experiencing a miracle—thanks to God's design for the eye.

The Bible asks an interesting question: "Does he who formed the eye not see?" (Ps. 94:9). A New Testament passage expands on that thought: "Nothing in all creation is hidden from God's sight. Everything is uncovered and laid bare before the eyes of him to whom we must give account" (Heb. 4:13). God sees and knows everything, and we cannot escape from the range of His vision. Whether this is good news or bad news depends upon you.

DOES IT MATTER?

Tiffany finished styling her hair and took an extra look at herself in the full-length mirror. She was satisfied—her new outfit would give her a few Monday morning compliments. Now that she'd finally been elected to student council and broken into the popular clique at school, she wanted to dress the part.

As she entered the building, Bob, the student council president, whistled at her. Marilee, a homecoming queen candidate, told her how nice she looked. Her day was off to a great start!

At lunchtime, she took her tray to the table where the popular senior girls sat. Two seats were available at the end. Looking across the room, she saw Alicia, a new girl that she'd met at church the day before. Tiffany gasped as she realized that Alicia was heading toward the empty seat next to her. Alicia wouldn't fit in with Tiffany's popular friends.

Besides, Alicia wore a "What Would Jesus Do?" bracelet—and Tiffany knew these popular girls thought that was very uncool. She was afraid that Alicia might start talking about church and blow her double life—"Tiffany, the super-Christian" on Sundays; Tiffany the worldly-wise, who, the rest of the week, went along with the crowd at school.

As Alicia approached, Tiffany snipped, "Sorry, this place is already taken." That was a lie, and Tiffany noticed that all during lunch, Alicia kept glancing at the empty chair.

During sixth hour, an office messenger brought Tiffany a note: "Please stop in the counselor's office after school." Wondering what was up, she headed for Mr. Baker's office after her last class. There sat Alicia!

"Come in," Mr. Baker motioned to Tiffany. "As a member of the student council hospitality committee, it's your turn to welcome a new student. This is Alicia Martinez, who just moved here from Los Angeles. I want you to give her a tour of the school and help her meet new friends." Tears welled up in Alicia's eyes.

VITAL INFORMATION

It shouldn't come as a shock when your sins come to light. It's easy to forget that God sees your every move and that His X-ray vision penetrates even your thought life.

Consider that "from heaven the LORD looks down and sees all mankind" (Ps. 33:13). If you assume that darkness will cover a nightlife that is displeasing to God, think again. Sin's consequences will come back to haunt you. If you compromise your principles to fit into non-Christian environments, sooner or later your behavior will come to light.

You'll also miss out on God's comfort, love, and care when you presume that God is far away and uninterested in the details of your life. God understands when your best intentions end in failure, and He is there, ready to encourage you when others make snide remarks or tell lies about you. He wants to clarify your doubts, eradicate your fears, and heal your broken heart. No place is outside the range of His vision.

THIS IS HOW TIFFANY'S LIFE COULD CHANGE IF SHE LISTENS TO GOD . . .

The words of a verse Tiffany had learned in Sunday school flashed across her mind: "Do not be proud, but be willing to associate with people of low position" (Rom. 12:16). Suddenly, she realized the ugliness of her arrogance and self-centeredness. Convicted of her sin, she breathed a silent prayer: *Lord, I'm really sorry. I've gone far from You. Please forgive me.*

A phone call distracted Mr. Baker from the awkward silence and the drama being played out in his office. Tiffany touched Alicia on the shoulder. "I owe you a big apology, Alicia," she said softly. "That seat next to me at lunch wasn't taken," she confessed. "I lied because . . . I was there with all the popular girls and . . . didn't want to be bothered."

Alicia silently nodded.

"Come with me . . . please . . . and I'll try to make it up to you." As they walked down the hall, Tiffany continued, "I can see that popularity was getting too important to me. I guess you could say I'd begun to worship it. I've not only hurt your feelings, but I lied to you . . . all because I didn't want the girls in my clique to know I was a Christian. Will you forgive me?"

Alicia smiled through her tears. "Yes, I forgive you."

"I think that God used you to show me what I've become. I wish I were brave like you, wearing a 'What Would Jesus Do?' bracelet . . . to a new school . . . on the first day. You don't seem to be afraid to let people know you're a Christian."

"Our school in L.A. was really tough," Alicia said. "Either you did a lot of bad things to fit in, or you had to suffer the consequences. My Christian friends and I made a decision—we'd let God use us to make the school different. We got a lot of teasing and even threats from gangs . . . but we got used to it."

Tiffany promised Alicia that they'd eat lunch together the next day. On Tuesday Tiffany introduced Alicia to her friends around the lunch table, but they all gave Alicia the cold shoulder.

After school, Marilee told Tiffany, "Alicia can't sit at our lunch table. She's only a junior."

That night Tiffany had to decide between Alicia and the popular clique. She cried and cried, but finally prayed, *Lord, I surrender my popularity to You. I'll do the right thing—no matter the price.*

When Tiffany's friends realized that she'd chosen to eat with Alicia instead of them, they all stopped talking to her. But Tiffany soon found that Alicia was an awesome friend.

Besides being thoughtful, kind, and unselfish, Alicia was transparent. And her close walk with God challenged Tiffany. Because both of her parents worked, Alicia always had to go straight home to watch her younger sisters and little brother, plus make dinner for the family. They lived in a small two-bedroom apartment, and Alicia had to give her parents the money she earned working Saturdays at her uncle's restaurant. Yet Alicia never complained. She had a great sense of humor and a zest for life that was contagious.

When Tiffany's mom was diagnosed with breast cancer, Alicia was there for her. She even took a city bus at night to come over and pray with Tiffany and her mom. Alicia's understanding and strong faith inspired Tiffany.

One day Jamie from the popular clique sat down to eat with Tiffany and Alicia. Tiffany was surprised, but said nothing. As they ate,

Jamie made small talk, gradually revealing the truth—Marilee had ostracized her from the group because Ken, the guy Marilee liked, had walked Jamie home. Tiffany breathed a silent prayer to God: "Thank you for rescuing me from such fickle 'friends.'"

The human eye is a miracle, but the Lord sees even more. The God who made the human eye sees everything. When Tiffany was running from God's will for her, she didn't like to reflect on that fact—and neither will you if you've got something to hide.

But if we genuinely want to follow Jesus—remembering that He is always present—we will be comforted, knowing that God is always watching, anxious to help us from going in the wrong direction. He's always there to correct us when we mess up, to encourage us when we're down, to answer our prayers when we're in trouble, to love us on yucky days, to forgive us when we fail, and to understand the desires of our hearts.

ACTION STEPS FOR LIVING WITH THE REALITY THAT GOD SEES EVERYTHING

1. Imagine God taking videos of all your actions, words, and thoughts. Then thank Him for His forgiveness, and determine to live in such a way as to receive rewards in heaven.
2. Remember that God is always right there to deliver you from temptation. Think of your greatest temptations and believe that Jesus is literally by your side as you face them.
3. Visualize Jesus taking your hand when you're discouraged, confused, afraid, or upset.
4. Enjoy His presence by sitting in stillness before Him.

WORDS TO LIVE BY

> The LORD is in his holy temple;
> the LORD is on his heavenly throne.
> He observes the sons of men;
> his eyes examine them.
>
> —Psalm 11:4

From his dwelling place he watches
all who live on earth—
he who forms the hearts of all,
who considers everything they do.
—Psalm 33:14–15

God has said, "Never will I leave you; never will I forsake you."
—Hebrews 13:5

12

THE UNIVERSE HAS A DIRECTOR

The universe appears to contain a lot of nothing. But appearances can be deceiving. Space is actually made up of about 72 percent hydrogen, 25 percent helium, and 3 percent heavier elements.[1]

Still, if you were to explore space in some sort of craft, your first impression would be how empty space is. An astronomer has estimated that space contains one atom for every eighty-eight gallons of space.[2]

In your space travels, you'd occasionally see a comet, which is "a loose collection of ice, rocks, and gravel surrounded by a cloud-like mass of very fine dust and gases that is sometimes blown backwards to form a glowing tail."[3] You'd also see some "space rocks" called asteroids and meteoroids. Finding a planet, though, would be difficult, because they are so rare.

While tooling around in your craft, you'd be wise to avoid black holes, because they can suck you right in. Black holes are collapsed remains of giant stars and are so dense that not even light can escape their awesome gravitational pull.[4] If a two-pound telephone directory were brought within twenty feet of a black hole, it would weigh more than one trillion tons.[5]

Your second impression would be how devoid of life space is. You wouldn't want to land on any of our solar system's neighboring planets.

Mercury's temperature ranges from 800 degrees Fahrenheit to minus 300 degrees Fahrenheit.[6] If you visited Venus without adequate protection, you'd suffocate while you were being crushed and fried. That's because there's nothing to breathe except carbon dioxide, the air pressure is nearly 100 times that of Earth, and the temperature is 900 degrees Fahrenheit.[7] The atmosphere on Mars isn't thick enough to sustain life,[8] and one of Jupiter's pleasant ten-hour days features 1,000-mile-per-hour winds.[9]

None of the eight other planets in our solar system is capable of supporting life, but with a high-powered telescope and by making an extensive search, you might locate some "evidence of life" on these planets. But it wouldn't mean that life originated there. It could have been transported there from the Earth, most likely when a meteorite struck our planet.

"Meteorites large enough to make a crater greater than 60 miles across will cause Earth rocks [some of which may contain fossil remains] to escape Earth's gravity. Out of 1,000 such rocks ejected, on average 291 will strike Venus, 20 will go to Mercury, 17 will hit Mars, 14 will make it to Jupiter, and one will go all the way to Saturn."[10]

Certain kinds of life forms—one-celled algae—have been found floating at altitudes ranging from 30,000 to 130,000 feet above the Earth. The sun's radiation exerts a pressure capable of carrying tiny life forms through our solar system, and there's enough graphite in space to protect them from harmful rays.

Some microorganisms can be kept at about minus 200 degrees centigrade for about six months without losing their ability to germinate.[11] So if you were to come across a once-living organism in our solar system, it's safe to assume that it originated on Earth.

Another impression you'd get on your space voyage is the vastness of space. Our galaxy alone, the Milky Way, contains over 200 billion stars—more recent estimates say 400 billion.[12] And it's estimated that there are more than one trillion galaxies.[13]

Stars are more than globs of hot gas. They make life possible. Large stars produce most life-essential elements in their thermonuclear furnaces.[14] Yet with approximately 70 sextillion stars (70,000 million million million, or seven with twenty-two zeros)—about ten times as many stars as there are grains of sand on all the world's beaches[15]—no known planet, other than Earth, even comes close to having the ability to support life.

So after your time in space, you'd be very glad to return to Earth, the only place in the universe where you'd be able to live.

It's amazing that God used the 110 elements[16]—things like iron, oxygen, hydrogen, helium—to create the entire universe—more than one trillion galaxies. He used those same elements to create giant blue whales, tiny goldfish, towering giraffes, chattering squirrels, stately palm trees, delicate orchids, geniuses like Einstein, and sweet little babies.

How could anyone but a divine Designer turn out such variety by using the same basic components? It should be obvious that Somebody outside the universe—Someone transcendent and made of different stuff than the 110 elements—created the heavens as well as human beings with their intelligence, creativity, talents, and diverse personalities.

DOES IT MATTER?

Mandy was furious. How could her parents be so old-fashioned?

She'd received an invitation to Kyle's "coming out of the closet" party, but her mom and dad told her that she couldn't go. Kyle lived next door, and Mandy had known him since she was five and he was eight. How could she not attend his party?

Her parents had always been kind to Kyle and included him in many of their family activities. Her dad often took him golfing with her brothers. "We can love Kyle," her father had explained, "without approving of everything he does. Someone has to take a stand in order to show him he's taking a wrong turn. I'll talk to him myself so you won't have to explain why you're not going to his party."

Mandy had to admit that she had loving and understanding parents, but why were they so far behind the times?

VITAL INFORMATION

The Bible describes the Creator of the universe as "the Lord God Almighty, who was, and is, and is to come" (Rev. 4:8).

And that constancy of God is reflected in nature. Gravity and momentum keep moons and planets in orbit; the sun, which rises so predictably each morning, is the same sun that Adam and Eve admired in the Garden of Eden; for centuries, people in different parts of the world have been able to count on breathable air—all sustained by our Creator. What would happen if God—with His total power—suffered from mood swings or repeatedly reversed His decisions? We can be thankful, though, that God is "unchangeable in His inner being, His attributes, His purposes, His motives of action and His promises."[17]

That does not mean that God doesn't allow us real freedom in our choices, nor does it imply that we can know ahead of time how God will respond in a given situation or to a particular request.

But because human decision-making, as well as God's responses to our prayers, stay within prescribed boundaries, we can have the security of the psalmist: "But you remain the same, and your years will never end" (Ps. 102:27). Although people's attitudes about right and wrong change with time and cultural influences, we can know that God will never change His mind about what is right and wrong, and we can exclaim with David, "Your word, O LORD, is eternal; it stands firm in the heavens" (Ps. 119:89).

IF MANDY REALIZES WHO GOD REALLY IS, HER ATTITUDE COULD CHANGE . . .

Mandy stayed home from Kyle's party because she had no other choice. But she resented her parents' trying to push their values on others. Then Mandy heard them express their disapproval of her cousin Jolene's morals.

Mandy faced her parents squarely. "That may be your truth, but it's not mine. If Jolene wants to move in with her boyfriend for this year at college, that's her decision. I'm sure she won't appreciate a lecture from her aunt and uncle."

"What's your definition of God?" her father asked abruptly.

"What does that have to do with this discussion?" countered Mandy.

"A lot more than you realize," said her father. "Who makes up the rules we should live by? Is it God, who always remains the same? Or is it popular opinion, which changes every decade?"

Mandy said nothing, but her expression remained adamant.

"Is God our Creator," her father continued, "and are we designed so that if we live according to His plan we'll be better off? Or did things spontaneously appear by chance so that what we do makes no difference?

"Does God know everything, which means that His wisdom stands forever? Or does the latest survey or scientific investigation determine truth?"

Mandy decided not to argue with her father. It never did any good. But she thought that the teachers in her public school knew a lot more than her parents did, and her teachers talked about morals changing with the times.

The school year passed slowly and Mandy welcomed spring. One Friday afternoon in May, she came home to find Jolene crying in her mother's arms.

"Why didn't I listen to you?" Jolene sobbed. "Why was I so blind?"

Jolene was pregnant, in spite of her using a contraceptive. The guy she thought she loved so much had moved in with another girl.

And the weekend had just begun. On Saturday Kyle—pale and visibly upset—stopped by the house.

"What's wrong?" asked Mandy's mother.

"It's Rand," Kyle said. "He's my current partner and . . . he's been diagnosed with AIDS. I'm afraid to get tested. When I first came out, you wanted me to . . . try a different path . . . and I was rude to you. But at least you showed you cared about me and . . . I know it's not fair for me to come to you now for help. But you're the only people I can trust."

Mandy's father put an arm around Kyle and said, "We'll do what we can to help you." Mandy's father talked to Kyle about places to find assistance, and he also talked to him about new life in Christ.

That evening, Mandy tried to study for a big chemistry test, but she couldn't concentrate. She realized that she was wrong and that her parents were right. A God who knows everything and never changes gave the commandments to protect the people whom He had created.

She shuddered, realizing the price she could have paid. She'd believed all the lies—that *right* changes, that the Bible was an outdated book, and that in modern times *right* might be different from what the Bible said was right in the past. Silently, she prayed, *Lord, forgive me for doubting your Word.*

Acknowledging the precision, power, and creativity of the Intelligence behind the stars will introduce you to the God who never changes or goes out of existence. He cared enough to make a hospitable planet for you to call home, and He made rules that are applicable in every century to ensure for you the best possible life.

Instead of calling your own shots, take your cues from the Director of the universe. He's looking out for your best interests.

ACTION STEPS FOR CELEBRATING THE GOD WHO IS ALWAYS THE SAME

1. Marvel at these facts:
   - The sun always comes up on time;
   - Spring always arrives;
   - The Earth rotates on its axis at precisely the correct angle;
   - The stars always appear at night;
   - You share these phenomena with Abraham, Alexander the Great, the apostle Paul, Christopher Columbus, and George Washington.
2. Some people think that Christianity is based on myth, and that all myths are equally valid. Imagine, though, what it would be like to worship a pantheon of Greek gods and goddesses. They pick favorites, have temper tantrums, punish for no reason, and

use humans as pawns in their fights with other gods. Then thank God that He is always the same.

3. Read through the Ten Commandments in Exodus 20:1–17. Add or subtract the word "not" to make each command say the opposite of what is written—for example, "You will kill"; "You will not honor your parents"; "You will not worship the Lord your God," and so forth. Think of what kind of society such rules would produce. Thank God for His rules.

4. If there's one of God's commands you'd rather not obey, think about your roller coaster emotions, uneven moods, and the frequency with which you change your mind. Compare that fickleness to God's constancy and faithfulness. Then ask yourself the question: "Who am I to talk back to God?"

WORDS TO LIVE BY

I will declare that your love stands firm forever,
   that you established your faithfulness in heaven itself.
                                                   —Psalm 89:2

Your word, O Lord, is eternal;
   it stands firm in the heavens.
Your faithfulness continues through all generations;
   you established the earth, and it endures.
                                         —Psalm 119:89–90

I the Lord do not change.

                                              —Malachi 3:6

PLUG INTO GOD'S SYSTEM

DID YOU KNOW?

Nature abounds with examples of interdependence among living things.

Your energy to play football, or study for an English test, or to hang out with your friends is dependent upon microorganisms that live in your intestines! These "good bacteria" break down molecules you couldn't otherwise digest. And in return, the bacteria get a nice warm home and a constant supply of food.[1]

Flowers and insects are another example of interdependent relationships. Flowers give insects nectar and insects help flowers to reproduce by spreading pollen. A honeybee travels an estimated 43,000 miles to produce just one pound of honey—so in the process spreads around a lot of pollen.[2]

When a hummingbird pushes its long bill inside a flower to extract nectar with its tube-like tongue, the top of its head is dusted with pollen. The bird then carries it to another flower.[3] It takes 1,600 blossoms to provide a hummingbird with its daily nectar,[4] so it, too, scatters a lot of pollen.

In the case of the Venus flytrap, the insect/flower interdependence takes a weird twist. The flower eats the insects. Once the flower's trap is sprung, it gradually pinches together, squeezing the victim against its digestive glands located on the surface of its leaves.[5] Doesn't that sound yummy?

Some ants in Central America live in nests that they hollow out in the pulp of the acacia tree. The ants eat the protein-rich nodules that grow at the tips of the leaves, and the tree thrives because the ants drive away all other predators.[6]

People and animals have an interdependent relationship with plants. The process of photosynthesis—by which plants use sunlight to produce carbohydrates from carbon dioxide and water—gives off oxygen for us to breathe. The carbon dioxide we exhale is used by plants.[7] Without plants, what would we eat? And what would the cows eat, and what would we, in turn, use to make hamburgers?

Other more fascinating examples of interdependence involve sea creatures. Large predatory fish swim the oceans, feeding on smaller fish and shrimp. Because the predator fish don't have toothbrushes, they need to deal with food residue and parasites in their mouths. No problem. They literally get in line at the nearest cleaning station, usually run by small bright-colored fish and certain shrimp. The giant fish open their mouths, exposing their vicious teeth, and the little cleaner fish swim right in to pick off all the parasites. When the job is done, the big fish lets them back out again—then swims away to find other little fish and shrimp to eat.[8]

Even more amazing is a bird called the Egyptian plover. It walks right into the open mouth of a Nile crocodile, cleans the croc's mouth, and afterwards comes out unharmed.[9]

It's hard to believe that time, chance, and the struggle for survival led to these interdependent relationships. It's more logical to believe they came about because of the plans and purposes of a master Designer.

The God who devised the interdependence we call the "balance of nature" also invented a system that enables people to live in peace. The person who considers the efficient functioning of nature wouldn't question the rightful authority that God has over us. If His commandments and His system of delegated authority are followed, the result for humans—as seen in these examples from nature—is harmony and successful living.

DOES IT MATTER?

Brett couldn't believe what was happening. Their new social studies teacher, Mr. Whitner, had brought a poster of the U.S. President to class, and he proposed that it be used as a dartboard. He cut up an American flag in front of the students and used one of the pieces to wipe down the shelves in the storage cupboard.

Next he asked a lot of questions:

"Why show respect for a piece of paper or a hunk of cloth?"

"Who says that marriage should be between a man and a woman?"

"Why should you obey the laws of the country, state, and city? Some people deserve to be killed. Some businesses make so much money they can afford to be robbed. And there are some good reasons why a person should drive fifty miles an hour in a thirty-mile-an-hour zone."

"Who has the right to tell you that abortion is wrong?"

"Why should you obey some army sergeant whose orders might get you killed?"

"Why do things a certain way just because it's tradition?"

Finally, Wade, the class brain, raised his hand. "You're advocating anarchy. Nobody wants to live in chaos with a complete absence of authority."

"Give me one good reason," Mr. Whitner shot back, "why I should obey another human who's no smarter than I am."

Wade didn't answer. Brett wondered if the idea of obeying authority was just something passed on through the generations and used to control people. His parents, his teachers, his boss at the burger place, and his government were restricting his freedom—and he didn't like it.

VITAL INFORMATION

Most would agree that the person best fit for the job should be given the position. What qualifications are necessary, then, for ruling the universe?

First, all authority should belong to the individual who created the world and its creatures. Only that individual knows how it would best function. The individual in a position of such power should be totally unselfish.

The possessor of all wisdom and knowledge—the Person who never goes out of existence—is the only One who can adequately govern the cosmos and make laws for its inhabitants.

God is, of course, the only one qualified to run the world. Besides having the intelligence and ability needed, He always has your best interests in mind—as well as that of the other six billion inhabitants of our planet.

Not only has God given us His rules in the Bible, He has also delegated limited authority—to representatives of government, Christian leaders, and parents. They are to be obeyed, provided that what they ask doesn't violate a biblical principle. A teen, for example, is justified in disobeying the parent who asks him or her to steal.

If, though, we're nothing more than a collection of molecules, submitting to authority makes no sense. Who's to say that any person's molecules are better than yours? Is it fair that any human—maybe the one with the most power or money, or the one with the best brain—could boss you around and have no one to answer to except himself or herself?

When the person in authority feels no responsibility to God, the world ends up with something like Hitler's Nazism or Stalin's Communism. Under that kind of authority, millions of innocent people lose their lives. For that reason, authority that isn't based on submission to God—and the commandments He has given—is indefensible.

IF BRETT FINALLY DECIDES TO LISTEN TO TRUTH, THIS MIGHT BE THE CONTINUATION OF HIS STORY . . .

Mr. Whitner's proud attitude made Brett angry. It was hypocritical for Mr. Whitner to say there's no basis for authority, and then make more demands on students than any other teacher in the school.

Mr. Whitner assigned students to answer the questions at the end of the chapter, requiring the answers to be submitted on a computer printout with the questions in red and the answers in black. Brett was furious. His color cartridge had run out of red ink the night before the assignment was due, and he had no way of getting another one in time.

Upon receiving Brett's paper, Mr. Whitner handed it right back, stating that Brett would receive a zero.

"I'm out of red ink," Brett said. "And to quote my social studies teacher, 'Give me a good reason why I should obey another human who's no smarter than I am.'"

The entire class broke out in applause and came to Brett's defense. Mr. Whitner barely survived until the bell rang, signaling the beginning of the weekend. On Monday, class seemed to have returned to normal—although tests and assignments were never returned.

A couple of months later, Brett's parents left town for a weekend convention, giving him strict orders not to leave the house for more than two hours at a time. A lot of robberies had occurred in the city, and Brett's mom was worried. They lived in a cul-de-sac where two homes were for sale and their closest neighbors were on vacation.

"Of course," Brett promised.

But when Daryl invited Brett on a day-long fishing trip, he couldn't resist. He hurried to get his stuff together, but at the last moment, he couldn't find the house keys. He searched everywhere.

Daryl's dad sat in the car outside, honking the horn. Brett figured he'd better leave or miss the trip. He closed the door without locking it and jumped into the car.

Returning at midnight on Saturday, he was horrified to discover that thieves had completely cleaned out their house—taking their furniture and everything they considered valuable. The police report indicated no sign of a break-in, and Brett couldn't hand over the house keys to his dad. The truth came out.

Brett doubted his parents would ever forgive him—and that was before the real shocker.

Brett was called into the counselor's office and informed by Ms. Selinsky that he wouldn't graduate because he'd flunked social studies. Brett was a B student, and he knew he'd gotten high grades on Mr. Whitner's tests. But the principal wouldn't even listen to his side of the story.

Brett's having to go to summer school and not being able to participate in graduation seemed like the end of the world. His decisions to defy authority certainly weren't working in his favor.

Brett retreated to his room, which was almost bare after the robbery. Lying on the floor in his sleeping bag, he flicked on an old radio that had been stored in the garage.

A guy was saying, "Maybe you've rebelled against authority and are paying the price. Perhaps you've experienced abusive authority."

Brett identified with what the man was saying.

"The only way to be at peace with authority is to submit completely to God's rightful authority over your life. He'll give you the power to obey. God has given others limited authority over you, and you are to obey as long as what others tell you to do doesn't go against God's greater authority. You can become rightly related to God through Jesus Christ, and stop beating your head against a brick wall by trying to go against God's rightful authority."

By now, Brett was ready to listen to this advice.

Think about the world that God created, with all its interdependent relationships. Remember that God's absolute authority—and the limited authority that He has delegated to others—have a purpose. It brings harmony and order to the universe.

We are, of course, free to ignore or defy the systems that God has put into place, but we'll suffer the consequences. Humans overrode God's balance of nature, for instance, when rabbits were introduced into Australia. There the rabbit had no natural enemies and the result was pure disaster. Australia is now overrun with rabbits, which do an enormous amount of damage. In the area of morals, God also put a system into place—a system of commandments. Disobeying them is risky. The failure to observe God's commandment to "flee from sexual immorality" (1 Cor. 6:18) has resulted in a huge percentage of young people becoming infected with incurable, sexually transmitted diseases.

God really does know best. Submitting to His authority will bring peace and contentment to your life.

ACTION STEPS TOWARD ACKNOWLEDGING GOD'S AUTHORITY

1. Realize that all of the Lord's commandments were made for our protection and blessing by an all-wise God. To disobey them is sin.
2. Face the reality that disrespect is always wrong, and that—unless you are asked to do something contrary to biblical principles—disobedience to teachers, bosses, government officials, and pastors is, in reality, rebellion against God Himself, because He has delegated authority to these people.
3. Use your extremely powerful weapon of prayer if an authority is unfair. When you obey an unreasonable but not antibiblical order and enlist God's justice, miracles can happen.
4. Stop pretending that you know how to run the universe better than God does, and stop verbally disrespecting His decisions.

WORDS TO LIVE BY

For rebellion is like the sin of divination [occult practices], and arrogance [is] like the evil of idolatry.

—1 Samuel 15:23

Everyone must submit himself to the governing authorities, for there is no authority except that which God has established.

—Romans 13:1

Give everyone what you owe him: . . . if respect, then respect; if honor, then honor.

—Romans 13:7

Children, obey your parents in the Lord, for this is right.
—Ephesians 6:1

Obey your leaders and submit to their authority.
—Hebrews 13:17

AUTOMATIC LIVING

Your body has six hundred muscles. They account for 40 percent of your weight, and give you the ability to move. As they work, your muscles burn a great deal of energy, which is produced from the foods that you eat. Most amazing, though, is the activity of the automatic muscles that control your eyelids, breathing, heartbeat, and digestion.

How good of God to make sure that we forgetful, scheming, and sometimes foolish humans can't interfere with these life-sustaining movements.[1]

Automatic movements help us breathe, something we all do about 23,000 times a day, 630 million times in an average life span. We take in more than one billion trillion molecules of air with each lungful,[2] which adds up to seven quarts of air every minute.[3] If weighed, all that air comes out to twenty-two pounds a day.[4]

Twenty-five percent of the oxygen we breathe in goes to the brain, 12 percent to the kidneys, and 7 percent to the heart.[5] Have you ever tried to see how long you can hold your breath? Before long, the accumulating carbon dioxide in your lungs will automatically trigger the muscles in your ribs, diaphragm, and lungs to move contrary to conscious desire[6]—and you'll take a breath.

Every minute, without any conscious effort on your part, the heart pumps blood through a 60,000-mile labyrinth of blood vessels inside of you—and then pumps it back.[7] Every day, your ten-ounce heart muscle contracts 100,000 times without missing a beat.[8] In a year, the average human heart circulates from 770,000 to 1.6 million gallons of blood through the body, enough to fill two hundred tank cars, each with a capacity of eight thousand gallons![9] In an average lifetime, the heart beats 2.5 billion times and pumps 60 million gallons of blood.[10]

Food digestion is just as miraculous. If one were to unravel the entire human alimentary canal—esophagus, stomach, large and small intestines—it would reach the height of a three-story building.[11]

Say you just ordered a pepperoni pizza, hold the anchovies. The average stomach has about a one-quart capacity, so there's a limit to how much you can eat and still feel comfortable. Throughout the day your stomach produces over three quarts of gastric fluid, including hydrochloric acid, which aids digestion. It's, in fact, remarkable that the stomach doesn't digest itself.

After the stomach, the next stop for the pizza is the small intestine, which produces enzymes to break down food, and has "a second brain" to supervise absorption. With an incredible number of fingerlike projections called villi and the even smaller microvilli, the overall absorption surface of the small intestine equals that of a tennis court.

Contributing to the way that pizza is used by the body is the liver. The football-sized, three-pound liver performs over five hundred functions, including the processing of all blood that leaves the stomach and intestines. The liver detoxifies substances, guards vitamins and minerals, stockpiles sugar for quick energy, and manufactures new proteins. The gall bladder, pancreas, and large intestine also make their contributions to digestion. Altogether, the entire digestive tract is 95 percent efficient—almost everything we eat is absorbed into the body.[12]

One could say that God wanted to stamp on the blueprint of the human body His rightful authority over life and death. As much as people insist they have total authority over their own bodies, no one, solely through an act of will, can stop a heart from beating, decide not to breathe, or order the stomach not to digest pizza calories.

God designed the human body to operate in spite of our own neglect or unhealthy choices. It's obvious, then, that life is a gift from God and not something to be devalued or discarded.

DOES IT MATTER?

In the darkness of his hospital room Tyler relived the nightmare of the last ten months. He and his girlfriend, Charmaine, told their parents they were going to a youth rally and out to eat afterward. Instead they went to a party at Adam's house.

Adam's parents were out of town, so liquor and drugs were plentiful. Tyler drank up—and he had little experience with alcohol. Then Charmaine looked at her watch and panicked. "I have to be home in fifteen minutes!"

Tyler drove as fast as he could. He didn't even slow down as he approached the railroad crossing. He saw the flashing red lights too late and was unable to stop in time. The influence of the alcohol in his bloodstream reduced his reaction time.

After days of unconsciousness, he awakened to a blur of pain, operations, and intensive care. When he was finally able to sit up, he was horrified to see that part of his left leg was missing. He cried in anguish, knowing that he'd never be able to go mountain climbing again. Everyone would stare at him if he wore shorts, and his dream of playing college tennis would never come true.

His left arm had also been damaged. In spite of three operations, the arm was not responding as it should. The doctor was kind but straightforward: "There's nothing more that we can do. If you're conscientious about physical therapy, you might regain 50 percent of the use in that arm."

When Tyler's thoughts at last turned from himself to Charmaine, the contradictory answers to his questions made him suspicious. One day his dad leveled with him—she had not survived the crash. Waves of guilt swept over Tyler. He had caused the death of the girl he loved.

Tyler couldn't see any reason to go on. The discussions his class had held in social studies made him doubt the existence of God. He remembered the conclusions they'd reached.

Charmaine had declared, "A baby conceived by accident should be aborted, because every child should be a wanted child." No one had objected. He and Charmaine had even decided—if they started having sex and she became pregnant, he'd take her to an abortion clinic. The class discussion about that scenario had resulted in a vote, and what he and Charmaine had agreed to do had been the most popular option.

The students also agreed that a sick, handicapped, or elderly person should have the right to assisted suicide, because of their reduced quality of life. Ms. Bianca had summed it up: "We're all accidents of evolution who report to no higher authority than ourselves. If a person's quality of life doesn't make living worthwhile, that person has a right to decide whether or not he or she wishes to remain alive."

A longing for death swept over Tyler, and he literally felt an evil presence urging him to commit suicide. He decided that as soon as he got home from the hospital, he'd drag himself to his parents' bathroom and down a whole bottle of his mother's sleeping pills.

VITAL INFORMATION

Your value doesn't depend upon how good-looking, smart, productive, or happy you are. Your worth comes from the fact that God created you especially to fulfill a unique purpose. And He loves you so much that He sent Jesus to die for you. When you feel you can't go on, He has miraculous strength and joy and comfort to give you.

Suicide is never the only way out because no problem is too big for God. Keep in mind that suicide is for keeps, destroying *all* your potential and inflicting permanent wounds on family and friends. Consider, too, that God designed your body for survival, even when it's under attack. So most suicide attempts are "unsuccessful," sometimes leaving the person with new health problems.

God tells us that He created us for His glory, and Jesus states: "I have come that they may have life, and have it to the full" (John 10:10). Don't miss out on what He has planned for you.

IF TYLER FOLLOWS THE ESCAPE ROUTE
GOD IS GIVING HIM, HIS STORY MAY
READ LIKE THIS . . .

Karissa's family had moved to the city from another state, and she got a job with the hospital food service. It was there that she heard about Tyler.

Sensing that God wanted her to reach out to Tyler, she asked the kids in her youth group for help. She and her brother Karl paid Tyler a visit in the hospital. At first he didn't respond much, but Karissa and Karl were persistent, often bringing other friends with them.

One day when Karl visited Tyler by himself, Tyler asked, "Do you think suicide is ever justified?"

"Have you thought of it?" Karl asked.

"Yes," Tyler heard himself say. "There's nothing to live for, and I don't like being a freak. I plan to take my mother's sleeping pills."

"I know your situation is tough," Karl said gently. "But God is a lot tougher. He can give significance to every life—especially," Karl looked Tyler square in the eyes, "when a person has accepted Jesus Christ as Lord and Savior. All of us can find hope, and we can experience His love. We're invited to plug into His power and be a part of something bigger than ourselves.

"So there's no reason to commit suicide. Yes, it's wrong for us to trash this gift of life that God has given to us. If the Lord meant for us to be in control of when we died, He would have created us with the ability to stop breathing or to keep our hearts from beating."

Karissa had gotten to know Tyler's mother and asked if the youth group could have a homecoming party for Tyler. They planned games Tyler could participate in, and the welcome home cake was as delicious as it was beautiful.

Tyler had to admit that he had a really good time. Everybody totally accepted him, and these kids had a joy he hadn't seen in any of his old friends. Tyler thought about all the work Karissa had done to give him such a neat party, and it brought tears to his eyes. He wanted to get to know God like those kids knew Him. For the first time since the accident, he felt that he might find something worth living for.

If thoughts of ending life have occurred to you or one of your friends, it's time to cooperate with God. He designed your body as an object lesson for the value of human life. Your heart keeps beating, your breathing is automatic, and your digestive system works on its own—whether you're awake or asleep.

God went to a lot of trouble to give you each day of life, and He wants you to discover His plan for each twenty-four-hour period. Join Tyler in deciding to let God give you meaning and purpose.

ACTION STEPS TO DEFEAT THOUGHTS OF SUICIDE (OR ABORTION)

1. Remember that the timeframe of your problem is only a millisecond compared with all eternity.
2. Don't make a permanent decision based on a temporary feeling. Look back to a situation you once thought was the end of the world, but today isn't such a big deal.
3. Realize that God has the right to decide life and death because He's the Creator, and because His overall plan is always best.
4. Consider that each thought of suicide or abortion has its source from the Devil, who loves death and is a master deceiver. It's a fact that you can submit yourself to God, "resist the devil, and he will flee from you" (James 4:7).
5. Reflect on the reality that God is all-powerful and all-loving, so He has a way out for you.

WORDS TO LIVE BY

The LORD brings death and makes alive;
he brings down to the grave and raises up.

—1 Samuel 2:6

You are precious and honored in my sight, . . .
everyone who is called by my name,
   whom I created for my glory,
   whom I formed and made.

—Isaiah 43:4, 7

He [God] himself gives all men life and breath and everything else.

—Acts 17:25

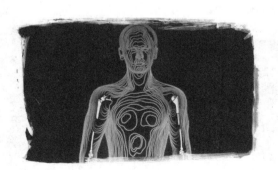

15

FEAR-BUSTING INFORMATION

Forty miles above the Earth is a layer of ozone. It literally is our lifesaver. Without it we would be burned, blinded, and broiled.

The ozone layer allows some of the sun's shorter ultraviolet rays—necessary for life on this planet—to pass through it, but screens out the sun's deadly, long ultraviolet rays. If these most deadly rays were to reach Earth, every living thing would die.

The ozone layer does, however, allow a tiny quantity of these more dangerous rays to pass through—just enough to kill most green algae. If these algae were allowed to grow uninhibited, they would completely fill all the lakes and rivers and oceans of the world, thus upsetting the balance of nature.

The atmosphere below the ozone layer is just as amazing. Air is 78 percent nitrogen, 21 percent oxygen, with the other 1 percent made up of almost a dozen trace elements, producing breathable air.[1] Our atmosphere is also "thin enough and of the right chemical composition to permit passage of light to the earth's surface."[2]

The Earth's atmosphere, then, is unduplicated. A lot of theories today proclaim that life originated in outer space, but so far not one planet has been found with an atmosphere capable of supporting advanced life.

Not only is Earth's atmosphere unique, so, too, is our planet itself.

By 2001, "astronomers had discovered fifty-two confirmed planets outside our solar system orbiting normal stars." (Which, like our sun, burn by changing hydrogen into helium by nuclear fusion.)[3] Although more planets are being found each year, by September 3, 2003, California and Carnegie Planet Search listed only 110 planets outside our solar system. Adding the nine in our solar system, the current total stands at 119.[4]

Compared with the trillions of stars, planets are scarce indeed. The 110 planets outside our solar system are all much bigger than our Earth. There may be many smaller ones, but they're harder to detect.

An age-old theory says a great number of stars, like our sun, have planets revolving around them—planets on which all the fine-tuned characteristics, including a breathable atmosphere for human life, may be present. That theory is proving to be incorrect.[5]

Only a small star—one similar to our sun—would be able to support life on a planet revolving around it. The star would also have to

- contain about the same amount of matter as our sun;
- find itself in the right star neighborhood;
- have the correct position in the galaxy;
- be the proper distance from a planet.

In addition, the planet itself would have to meet many strict specifications, including

- correct surface temperature;
- correct surface gravity;
- correct atmospheric composition and pressure;
- correct rotation rate;
- a stable rotation axis tilt.[6]

The vast majority of stars just don't have planets, let alone planets that could support life. "Not only are planetary systems relatively rare, [but] of the systems that do exist, few, if any, are like our solar system."[7]

All this means that God designed every detail of our solar system just so we could enjoy our lives on Earth. Astronomer Hugh Ross sums it up:

> The remoteness of the probability of finding a planet fit for life suggests that the Creator personally and specifically designed and constructed our galaxy group, our galaxy, our sun, Jupiter, . . . the moon and Earth for life.[8]

It would take immense credulity to believe that life on Earth actually began in outer space. Besides the lack of a suitable environment for life somewhere in space, other questions pop up:

- How did life begin?
- Who or what provided the materials from which it was made?
- How did the material get transported to our planet?

So enjoy your next breath—and be thankful for all the other conditions that make planet Earth a place you can call home. Be thankful, too, that you live on the only known planet where breathing *is* possible.

It's highly unlikely that the God who took so much care in creating a special place for you to live is incapable of handling your fears and anxieties. It's absurd, in fact, to think that the Creator of the universe can't help you weather your present crisis. The God who took care to create all the conditions necessary for your life *will* watch over you.

Just as the ozone layer protects the Earth and ensures the balance of nature, God watches over those who belong to Him. He sometimes allows trials and problems to keep us mindful of our dependence upon Him, but He sticks with us during our lives here until it's time to go to heaven and live with Him.

DOES IT MATTER?

Vanessa was still in a state of shock. Brittany's locker was right next to hers. After school on Friday, Brittany had loaned Vanessa her biology notes, and they had talked about their weekend plans.

Brittany's plans never took place. The Saturday morning news said that her body had been found in the river. She had been raped before she'd been brutally stabbed. No one was sure what had actually happened.

But Vanessa knew Brittany. She was not a wild girl who took unnecessary chances.

Her parents said she had left home at 4:40 Friday afternoon for the fifteen-minute walk to her work place, and she was scheduled to start work at 5:00. They knew she usually took the shortcut through the park, which was considered very safe. But she never arrived at work.

Now Vanessa had nightmares. Often she thought she heard footsteps behind her. She looked around but never saw anyone. She experienced a constant fear that she just couldn't shake. She was afraid to be alone, and no place seemed safe.

VITAL INFORMATION

How can Vanessa—or you—deal with the insecurities and the real dangers in this world?

Remember that the all-loving and all-powerful God has spread an ozone "net" over us to screen out what is harmful and transmit what is necessary. He can be trusted, then, to care for us in all circumstances. We have the Lord's promise: "He [or she] who dwells in the shelter of the Most High will rest in the shadow of the Almighty. I will say of the LORD, 'He is my refuge and my fortress, my God, in whom I trust'" (Ps. 91:1–2). He is faithful.

IF VANESSA LOOKS FOR GODLY ADVICE AND DECIDES TO FOLLOW IT, HER STORY COULD CONTINUE SOMETHING LIKE THIS . . .

Vanessa opened her biology notebook to study for the test. Out fell the notes that Brittany had loaned to her. Vanessa just stared at them. Her mind wandered back to Brittany's funeral, the trauma of experiencing for the first time the death of a person her own age, and the sudden realization of the uncertainty of life.

She and her friends had done a lot of crying. She recalled the eerie feeling that swept over her the next day at school when she looked over at Brittany's locker. Brittany would never open it again, or say hi to her in the hall, or ace another biology test. Now Brittany's notes seemed like something sacred. Maybe she should give them to Brittany's mother.

Vanessa had had another nightmare the day after the funeral. She dreamed that a monster man with a huge butcher knife was trying to catch her. And she woke up screaming.

She was still afraid to walk alone anywhere. Although she never mentioned it, she dreaded being at home by herself—even for a few minutes. Since studying was now impossible, she decided to confide in her mother.

"Mom, can I talk to you?"

"What is it, sweetheart?" her mother asked as she turned off the TV.

Vanessa started to cry. "It's what happened to Brittany. I'm afraid all the time, and I can't seem to get over it."

Vanessa's mom motioned to her and they sat next to one another on the sofa.

"When I was your age," her mother said, "a popular guy from my high school was killed in a car accident. I was terrified of dying because I'd never made things right with God. Honey," her mother said, looking Vanessa in the eye, "are you sure that if you died tonight you'd go to heaven?"

"I'm not positive."

Her mother explained that assurance was possible. Then she asked Vanessa if she was willing to repent of her sin, turn from it, and totally give her life to Jesus.

Because Vanessa was ready to do just that, her mother led her in a short prayer, asking God's forgiveness and inviting Jesus to control Vanessa's life as her Savior and Lord.

"Once you're certain you'll go to heaven," her mother said, "part of the fear is conquered. But God also expects us to cooperate with Him in using common sense and avoiding unnecessary risk. Grab the Bible on the coffee table and read Proverbs 27:12."

Vanessa found the passage and read it out loud. "The prudent see danger and take refuge, but the simple keep going and suffer for it."

"You're doing a great job of seeing the danger," her mother said and smiled, "but there's another part of the equation—a command found many times in the Bible: 'Fear not.' Why don't you look up Psalm 56:3?"

Finding her place, Vanessa read, "When I am afraid, I will trust in you."

Her mother walked her through an illustration. "Imagine a strong father with his little girl in his arms. She's hysterical because of the barking cocker spaniel at her father's feet. This father can in good conscience order, 'Ramona, stop crying. The puppy can bark loud, but he can't hurt you while I'm protecting you.'

"Our heavenly Father, who has infinite power to protect us from all harm, has the right to ask us not to be afraid . . . because He has everything under control. Either He will protect us totally or give us the strength we need for a difficult situation . . . or take us straight to heaven. Whatever happens, He is there."

"Thanks, Mom," Vanessa said. "But I want you to do something for me."

"What is it?"

"Christy's mom prays with her each morning before she leaves the house, asking for God's protection. Will you do that for me?"

"That's a great idea!" her mother exclaimed. "Why didn't I think of it myself?"

God knows how to allow only a few harmful rays to pass through the ozone layer—the ones that will prevent a destructive overgrowth of algae. In the same way, He will never permit any situation in your life that He will not mold for good—if you give it to Him—in His time-plus-eternity plan. But when the problems come, rather than trying to handle them alone, choose to trust Him and receive the comfort and solutions He has for you.

ACTION STEPS TO CONQUERING FEAR

1. Make sure of your salvation, so that you know that death will only open the door to a fantastic forever.
2. Take reasonable precautions and avoid unnecessary risks.
3. Look up these "fear not" verses, memorize them, and take them literally:
    * Psalms 4:8; 27:1–2; 34:4, 7; 57:1–3; 91:2–15
    * John 14:27
    * Hebrews 13:5–6
4. Find someone to pray with you about conquering your fear.

WORDS TO LIVE BY

For the LORD God is a sun and shield;
   the LORD bestows favor and honor;
no good thing does he withhold
   from those whose walk is blameless.

       —Psalm 84:11

If you make the Most High your dwelling—
   even the LORD, who is my refuge—
then no harm will befall you,
   no disaster will come near your tent.
For he will command his angels concerning you
   to guard you in all your ways.

       —Psalm 91:9–11

So do not fear, for I am with you;
   do not be dismayed, for I am your God.
I will strengthen you and help you;
   I will uphold you with my righteous right hand.

       —Isaiah 41:10

16

YOU'RE NOT MISSING A THING

The human body contains ten to the twenty-eighth power (10^{28}) atoms (that's a one followed by 28 zeros).[1] For comparison, that would be more than the number of grains of sand on all the world's beaches.[2]

Atoms are the fundamental particles that constitute cells, and your body contains between 10 trillion and 100 trillion cells.[3] Many cells live less than a day, red blood cells live four months, and certain muscle cells will live for years.[4]

Each cell has about one trillion atoms that are constantly being torn down, remodeled, and replaced.[5] Cumulatively, in your lifetime, for example, you'll grow almost 100 feet of fingernails.[6] Every couple of days you replace all the cells that line the intestinal tract.[7]

Ninety percent of the atoms in your body, then, are replaced every year, and every five years 100 percent of your atoms are replaced.[8] In the last hour one trillion trillion of your atoms have been replaced—along with a lot of cells.[9] David M. Bougham, M.D., explains it like this: "We are continually being recreated from dust and returning to dust."[10]

Because the body is self-building, self-regulating, self-repairing, and knows how to convert food into energy, Scottish biologist Sir J. Arthur Thomson calls it "the most marvelous and unique automatic mechanism in the universe."[11]

These fundamental particles of which we are made have been floating around since Creation and are constantly being exchanged among neighbors—even crossing international boundaries. One of your atoms could someday inhabit someone from Afghanistan.

Yet you continue to be you and your body hangs together—even though the rate of atomic turnover within you is so rapid it would require every person on the planet to count ten billion atoms per second to keep up with it all.[12] Unaware of this miraculous and painless process, you just go about your life.

Physicist John Tyndall sums it up: "Life is a wave, which in no two consecutive moments of its existence is composed of the same particles."[13]

The whole universe, at the atomic level, is in the process of change, and the amazing complexity of maintaining life on earth requires a force outside of the universe, transcending it.[14] If someone could conceive of Earth without a Creator, God would have to be invented just to keep it going. Only an all-powerful and all-intelligent God could have maintained for century after century all the complicated processes and delicately balanced natural systems.

It's amazing, however, that even people who acknowledge the greatness and awesomeness of God insist on being self-sufficient. If we all were honest, we'd have to plead guilty to trying to solve our own problems, pooling our ignorance with other humans to decide how life should be lived. It's all too easy for us to think we can run our lives better than God can, and that our preferences are more important than the rules He made for our own good.

DOES IT MATTER?

Dallas exploded. "Why did I get stuck with the strictest and most old-fashioned parents on the planet?" He stomped into his bedroom and slammed the door. All he had done was ask if he could go camping with Kent and his family.

"You only met Kent two months ago," his mother argued. "We don't know the Andersons, so we have no idea what kinds of things you'd be exposed to."

"Besides," his father stated, ending the discussion, "Pastor Brian has planned a special seminar for youth on Saturday, and I don't want you to miss it."

Dallas felt hemmed in. He wanted new experiences, different friends, and most of all, he wanted to fit in at school. To him, most of the church kids were too serious. He felt his folks still treated him like a child. He wanted to make his own decisions and live his own life.

Kent was a new kid at school. He had an incredible sense of humor and a love of life, which meant that things were never boring when he was around. An observation Kent had made in their social studies class one day sounded logical. "Why should we stop having fun just because an old book that's been around for centuries tells us to honor our parents? Modern psychologists say that we should express ourselves and let our true feelings out. We can't expect our parents to understand us. *They* grew up in the dark ages."

VITAL INFORMATION

God really does know everything. Every facet of nature spells out God's credentials as being smart enough and having the right to tell you what to do.

In the Bible, He actually presents you with a map for not getting lost, and gives instructions on how to keep from messing up your life. Joshua 1:8–9 gives a great promise: "Do not let this Book of the Law depart from your mouth; meditate on it day and night, so that you may be careful to do everything written in it. Then you will be prosperous and successful. Have I not commanded you? Be strong and courageous. Do not be terrified; do not be discouraged, for the LORD your God will be with you wherever you go."

How foolish to follow the path that says, "There is a way that seems right to a man, but in the end it leads to death" (Prov. 14:12), instead of choosing the option that promises, "The fear of the LORD is the beginning of ... wisdom" (Prov. 1:7).

IF DALLAS PAYS ATTENTION TO GOD'S WARNING SIGNS, THE NEXT CHAPTER IN HIS LIFE COULD READ LIKE THIS . . .

Dallas sulked his way through the whole weekend, hoping that Monday would be more exciting. Like a robot, he walked to school, attended his first four classes, and headed toward the lunchroom. On the way, he saw Kent at his locker.

"Hey, Kent, how was—"

Kent turned around, and Dallas gasped. Kent had a horrible black eye.

"What on earth happened to you?" Dallas exclaimed.

Kent glanced around to make sure no one else was nearby. "Just some . . . trouble at the campground," he said, not meeting Dallas's eyes.

"Hey, Kent, it's me, Dallas. C'mon . . . you can trust me."

Kent hesitated, then the whole story spilled out.

"Well . . . my dad and my uncle started drinking big time. And when my dad's drunk, he gets really mean. He started beating up my mom. I couldn't call the police from way out at the campground, so I had to defend her. I was able to protect my mom, but I got a black eye in the process. That happened Friday night. My mom and I hitched a ride to the nearest town. We found the bus depot and came back Saturday morning. But my dad still hasn't come home. He's probably at my uncle's house."

"I'm sorry, Kent," Dallas said. He didn't know what else to say. He'd never been this close to someone who had such a troubled family life.

Kent sighed. "Yeah . . . well . . . when your dad's an alcoholic, that's just the way things are." Kent laid a hand on Dallas's arm. "You can't tell anyone what happened, because my dad might do something drastic."

"Like I said," Dallas placed his hand on Kent's shoulder, "you can trust me."

As they ate lunch in silence, Dallas came to his senses.

He had parents who loved him and looked out for him, and he

didn't appreciate it. He knew God's principles for finding real peace, and he was rebelling against them.

Dallas now realized that Kent's great personality was his attempt to mask reality. Right there, Dallas breathed, "Lord, I was wrong. Please forgive me," and he decided to turn his life completely over to the Lord.

That night Dallas apologized to his parents. Telling them the whole story, he asked for their forgiveness. He then asked if Kent could go with them river rafting the next weekend. His parents agreed, and everyone had a wonderful time.

"I can't believe your parents," Kent said. "They act like they love each other, and they're so polite about giving orders to you and your brothers."

Kent spent more and more time at Dallas's house. One night he called and asked if he could stay the night because his mother was out of town and his dad had invited his drinking buddies over for a party.

Soon Kent seemed like a member of the family—and his ideas and habits were changing. He started attending the youth group and going to church with Dallas and his family. The day Kent accepted Christ, Dallas's father invited him to join them at a nice restaurant after church so they could all celebrate.

As they were riding home in the minivan, his father flipped on a praise CD. Everyone listened or sang along. Dallas thought about how close he'd come to throwing his Christian heritage overboard because he wanted to experience "the world." From Kent, he learned that he hadn't missed a thing.

The God who supervises the complicated process of constantly replacing atoms in your body can be depended upon to give commandments that will best ensure your safety, health, and happiness. The One who maintains the universe knows how to make your future the best it can be. Trust Him.

ACTION STEPS WHEN YOU'RE TEMPTED TO GIVE UP ON BIBLICAL CHRISTIANITY

1. Don't allow a few hypocrites to keep you from Jesus. He's perfect.
2. When faced with rules that seem unreasonable, politely ask to see the Scripture passage on which the prohibitions are based. Read the Bible for yourself. You can reject someone's incorrect interpretation of the Bible or nonbiblical ideas without turning away from God and His Word.
3. Read testimonies of people who have rebelled against God. Talk to those who've rebelled before accepting Christ, and ask them if it was worth it.
4. Ask yourself, "Does it make sense to go against the principles of the God who made me, who loves me, and who knows everything?"

WORDS TO LIVE BY

Do not conform any longer to the pattern of this world, but be transformed by the renewing of your mind. Then you will be able to test and approve what God's will is . . . his good, pleasing and perfect will. Love must be sincere. Hate what is evil; cling to what is good.

—Romans 12:2, 9

If our gospel is veiled, it is veiled to those who are perishing.
—2 Corinthians 4:3

GETTING BACK ON TRACK

Without the moon, life on Earth would be impossible. The moon's gravitational force creates the tides that cause the waves to break continually on the ocean shores. The tidal effect mixes oxygen, nitrogen, and trace elements of our atmosphere, thus providing us with a constant supply of oxygen. This process also causes air to circulate through the seas, providing oxygen for plankton—the microscopic plant and animal life—which floats in bodies of water and, either directly or indirectly, supplies food for the fish. The fish in turn supply food for the birds, animals, and people.[1]

Without plankton, there would not be enough oxygen—and we all need to breathe. Microscopic plants, called phytoplankton, produce "at least 80% of the oxygen we breathe." Some scientists calculate that without the oxygen production of phytoplankton, life as we know it could not exist.[2]

The tidal movements caused by the moon also remove the garbage and gunk from oceans and shores. If it weren't for the moon, you'd have to wear nose plugs when you're trying to get a suntan at the beach.[3]

God made the moon just the correct size and placed it a suitable distance from the Earth to perform these and other functions. If, for example, the moon were much closer to the Earth, tidal effects on the Earth's oceans, atmosphere, and rotation rate would be too severe. If the moon were much farther from the Earth, tides would be too low to move nutrients through the oceans and between the continents. The moon's location also affects our weather. A change in the angle of the moon's orbit would cause instability in the Earth's climate.[4]

Here are some other interesting moon facts to ponder.

- The diameter of our moon is 2,160 miles—a little more than one-fourth that of Earth.[5]
- The Earth has eighty-one times more mass than the moon.[6]
- The moon is an average of 238,870 miles away from us and orbits the Earth every 29.53 days.[7]
- Moon temperatures vary from 266 degrees Fahrenheit to minus 292 degrees Fahrenheit.[8]

The moon adds much more than just beauty, then, to your existence. The entire natural universe, in fact, maintains its balance and connectedness because each part functions as God designed. In a similar way, God has set in place principles that must be observed in order for us to have a right relationship with Him and to interact successfully with other people. Be thankful for both God's natural and moral principles.

DOES IT MATTER?

Garret couldn't believe the mess that his wrong choices had created. It all started when he and Todd decided to attend the football team's end-of-the-season "kegger." To avoid being questioned by his parents, Garret had arranged to spend the night with Todd, since his mom was less strict.

They found Todd's mom after the game and told her they were going to town to have hamburgers with the other kids to celebrate the victory and might be a little late. Both felt sort of guilty about lying, but they wanted to fit in with the popular guys.

Todd drove his car to the woods where the beer party was to take place. They didn't intend to drink much and planned to leave early.

What they didn't know was that the local TV station was doing a special report on teenage drinking and had been tipped off about the party. A young cameraman and a reporter had approached unnoticed and managed to do quite a bit of filming before somebody screamed a warning. Garret and Todd ran for the car.

The footage appeared on the "In Depth" part of the local news later that evening. Garret and Todd, beer in hand, appeared on the screen in living color.

Making matters even worse, just that morning the publicity had been sent out for the ladies' luncheon. Todd's mother was to speak there on "Biblical Parental Guidance in a Teen's Life."

VITAL INFORMATION

What can Garret do? And what recourse do you have when your own wrongdoing messes up your life?

God, who created the moon to clean up this planet and who constantly directs that complicated process, has put in place a way for you to be cleansed and forgiven. He will guide you in putting your life back on track. Doing so will require total honesty, a willingness to humbly ask God and others for forgiveness, a determination to try to make things right, and a new resolve to obey God.

IF GARRET DECIDES TO RESPOND POSITIVELY TO GOD AND HIS WORD, THE STORY MIGHT CONTINUE LIKE THIS . . .

Garret's parents were waiting for him at Todd's house. His mother was crying and his father tersely explained the TV clip, concluding, "I'm too angry to talk now. I might say something I shouldn't."

They rode home in silence, and Garret went to his room in a daze.

The next morning, when he made his way to the kitchen for some breakfast, Garret overheard his mother talking on the phone.

"I never thought my son would plan to disobey the law and lie to cover it up. Garret has betrayed my trust." Breaking into tears, she sobbed, "How can I ever face those women at the luncheon?"

Feelings of guilt and regret overwhelmed Garret. A verse he'd memorized came to his mind: "If we confess our sins, he is faithful and just and will forgive us our sins" (1 John 1:9). He hurried to his room to pray and to ask the Lord to forgive him.

He knew he also had to talk to his mother. Feeling awkward and unsure of himself, each step between his room and the kitchen seemed like a giant effort. He felt as if one of those little demons—that sit on people's shoulders in cartoons—were whispering in his ear, "Aw, just forget it and go on with your life. Most kids experiment with alcohol. It's no big deal."

But he crept into the kitchen and blurted out, "Mom, I'm sorry. Will you forgive me?"

His mother placed her arm around him and responded, "Of course."

A feeling of relief swept over Garret. But like the scars that remain after a serious wound, there were consequences of sin for Garret to face. He dreaded school on Monday, knowing that a lot of people would mention that they'd seen him on TV. He knew he'd be teased, and it would be much easier to say something like, "You've got to get famous somehow," and brush off the whole thing. That attitude would make him a hero of sorts.

But Garret had decided—if someone said something, he'd respond, "It wasn't right, and I'm sorry I did it."

Monday morning was the nightmare he anticipated, but he stuck to his decision and knew he'd gained a victory.

Dark circles under his mother's eyes, however, indicated that she was having trouble sleeping. His father reacted by establishing his own FBI—the "Family Bureau of Investigation." Garret had to report his every move, and one of his parents always checked his whereabouts with a phone call. They cut half an hour off his curfew and picked him up after athletic events.

He felt like lashing out and complaining that he was being treated like a little kid. But he realized that he needed to regain their trust, so he decided to cooperate. Instead of accusing his mother of worrying too much, he wrote her a couple of notes to tell her how much he appreciated her.

His parents were suffering embarrassment and extra stress because of his actions. He knew that Chelsey, the girl he most wanted to impress, had lost her respect for him. She didn't say anything, but he could tell by the look in her eyes that he'd disappointed her.

He wondered how Jesus felt. He had to make sure that nothing like this ever happened again.

The real reason he and Todd had gone to the "kegger" was because Darren—Mr. Popularity himself and next year's football captain—had personally invited them—and Darren's friends automatically joined the cool crowd at their school. Todd and Garret desperately wanted to be part of that group.

Garret had to decide between popularity and God. He finally chose God, knowing that it would cost him a lot. But it would be worth it; a clear conscience and a right relationship with the Lord were more important than being accepted by Darren and his clique.

You, along with Garret, can make plans to "plug the holes"—to surrender to God the desires and attitudes that open you to specific temptation. Be on your guard so you don't sin in the same way again.

Forgiving us and placing us on the right path again are among God's most wonderful provisions for helping us clean up our act—even better than the "moon-maid" planetary cleaning service! Take advantage of forgiveness and correction each time you sin against the Lord. But remember that honesty and humility are prerequisites for God's forgiveness.

ACTION STEPS FOR MAKING A COMEBACK AFTER SINNING

1. Confess what you did to God—without making excuses.
2. Accept His forgiveness.
3. Apologize to those you have wronged.
4. Live humbly with the consequences of your wrongdoing.

WORDS TO LIVE BY

Wash away all my iniquity
    and cleanse me from my sin. . . .
Against you, you only, have I sinned
    and done what is evil in your sight. . . .
Create in me a pure heart, O God,
    and renew a steadfast spirit within me. . . .
Restore to me the joy of your salvation
    and grant me a willing spirit, to sustain me.
                —Psalm 51:2, 4, 10, 12

You are forgiving and good, O Lord,
    abounding in love to all who call to you.
                —Psalm 86:5

18

HAVE IT GOD'S WAY

DID YOU KNOW?

It's hard to fit the facts into the theory—the theory of evolution, that is, which many people accept as true. Evolutionists proclaim that life began as a single cell and progressed through trial and error, evolving and branching out quite systematically into more complex life forms. But it would be impossible to guess what, for example, the platypus of Australia evolved from or what it's evolving into.[1]

The platypus has a bill and webbed feet like a duck—except that it has four legs and when on land, the webbing of the front feet folds into its palms so it can walk or dig more efficiently. It has fur like an otter, a tail like a beaver, and no "proper" ears.[2]

When it hunts for shrimp, worms, frogs, tadpoles, snails, or small fish under water, its "eyelids" close, also covering its ear holes. Using electric sensors in its bill to pick up the minute electrical charges that all living things emit, the platypus easily locates its prey,[3] which it then stores in cheek pouches like a chipmunk. Instead of teeth, an adult platypus has grinding pads with shearing edges.

The platypus lays one to three leathery eggs at a time, and the bean-sized, hairless babies feed on milk that oozes from pores in the mother's body, much like a kangaroo.[4]

The male platypus is the sole species of mammal equipped with "specialized poison glands" similar to that of many reptiles. The poison is in a small sac[5] connected to a hollow claw-like spur behind the ankle of the platypus.[6] In clinical trials, the venom—similar to the poison of some snakes—causes a rapid decrease in blood pressure and eventual death in, for example, rabbits.[7]

The uniqueness of the platypus isn't, however, the only thing that gives evolutionists a headache.

Hemoglobin is a complex, iron-rich protein molecule in the red blood cell, and it carries oxygen from the lungs to the tissues. The hemoglobin in each red blood cell of humans, for example, allows it to carry one million molecules of oxygen.[8] The building blocks of hemoglobin are called amino acids. "It has been calculated that the chance that amino acids would line up randomly to create the first hemoglobin protein is 10^{850}."[9]

Complete and fully functioning hemoglobin molecules are found not only in humans but also in most animals with backbones, some earthworms, some starfish, some clams, some insects, and even in some bacteria. There seems to be no traceable pattern as to why some creatures ended up with hemoglobin and others did not![10]

Other examples defy the "evolutionary ladder." Darwin wrote, "To suppose that the eye [with so many parts working together] . . . could have formed by natural selection, seems I freely confess, absurd in the highest degree."[11] Darwin likely would have been even more amazed if he'd known about the eye of an octopus. It's similar to the human eye and in some ways superior. Octopuses can pick out finer details than humans can and see better in dim light.[12]

Another example that might leave evolutionists scratching their heads is a protein called lysozyme. Tests show that the lysozyme in chickens is more like that of humans than that of any living mammal.[13]

Evolutionists assume that similarities among living things prove that they all came from the same single cell, which evolved into many life forms. But consider that "flying fish" actually *leap* into the air at up to twenty miles per hour. They use their wide pectoral fins as wings to soar as high as twenty feet and as far as 1,300 feet in one glide.[14] Yet no one seriously suggests that birds evolved directly from these fish.

Isn't it more logical to conclude that similarities between less complex and more complex creatures mean they all were made by the same Designer? Any good engineer understands the principle of using ideas that work in one structure to create another—even though the two resulting structures may look different from one other. Assuming that what appears to be less complex necessarily gives rise to the more complex can lead to illogical conclusions like "the car evolved from the skateboard."

Instead of believing that living things are products of natural causes and must, therefore, fit into some evolutionary ladder, why not credit their creation to God? He created an orderly universe that functions with precision, revealing His faithfulness. The universe He created continually provides us with mysterious and marvelous new discoveries, reminding us of His greatness.

What He does and the way He carries out His plans and purposes defy human explanation and understanding. This principle also applies in the spiritual dimension. Religions invented by humans grade on performance—meditation, praying five times a day, following dietary rules, knocking on doors, doing good deeds, protecting the environment, and so forth. But God's idea for rescuing us was to send His Son to pay the penalty of sin, making salvation available by grace, through faith, to all who believe.

DOES IT MATTER?

It was Easter week and Jillian invited Emily to the special drama at her church.

"I guess I should give it to you straight," Emily sermonized. "I just don't get excited by yearly reminders of a man who was put to death because he wasn't smart enough to outwit his enemies."

"But Jesus died for our sins," Jillian objected, "so that we can accept God's free gift of salvation and go to heaven."

"Give me a break," Emily shot back. "If there is a God, He'll recognize intellectual honesty, hard work, and contributions to humanity. I'm better than most people, so I'll have no problem."

"If there is a God," said Jillian, "and I believe there is, isn't it dangerous to assume that your method of getting to heaven is better than His? Your formula for salvation is exactly the opposite of the information found in the Bible. God gave us the Bible to tell us His requirements."

"My dad's here to pick me up," Emily interrupted, "and he doesn't like to wait." Emily hurried toward the black Lexus.

As she waited for her ride, Jillian decided she'd have to pray even harder for Emily.

VITAL INFORMATION

God is the Author of salvation. Isaiah 43:10–11 states: "Before me no god was formed, nor will there be one after me. I, even I, am the LORD, and apart from me there is no savior."

That Jesus is the Savior is one of the strongest arguments for believing He came to the earth as God in human flesh. It's presumptuous, ridiculous, and dangerous to assume that there's another way to heaven that is different from the one God laid out for us: "This righteousness [being given credit as if we'd lived up to God's standards] from God comes through faith in Jesus Christ to all who believe. There is no difference, for all have sinned and fall short of the glory of God, and are justified freely by his grace [undeserved benefit] through the redemption [ransom price for sin] that came by Christ Jesus" (Rom. 3:22–24).

Modern life is full of contradictions. In our culture, people want to live by simple slogans—"You get what you pay for," "There's no free lunch," and "No pain, no gain"—but at the same time conclude that eternal salvation is based upon a complex mixture of good works, good intentions, and faulty logic.

God is at liberty, however, to use a different standard when it comes to spiritual life. He has done just that—all because no amount of human effort can enable anyone to perfectly keep all of God's commandments. For this reason, salvation is a gift given only to those who are humble enough to receive it.

IF JILLIAN PERSEVERES IN PRAYER
AND MAINTAINS A CARING FRIENDSHIP
WITH EMILY, THIS COULD BE THE
OUTCOME . . .

Emily was chosen to head a special student council committee. Their group would raise money for a reputable charity that was helping flood victims. With characteristic energy and dedication, Emily organized fundraisers and collected individual donations.

Two days after she started the project, her dad got fired from his high-paying job. The next day, Hans, the guy she dreamed about night and day, invited her to the prom.

Jillian helped with a couple of fundraisers and listened as Emily described her prom dress and the outfits she'd bought for the graduation banquet and the honor society installation. Jillian wondered where Emily got the money to go to the city and shop in the most expensive stores—now that her father was unemployed—but she said nothing.

Emily's picture was in the paper as class valedictorian, and she was awarded a huge scholarship. But, behind the scenes, things were falling apart. Mr. O'Connor, the student council advisor, questioned the amount on the receipt that the student committee had received from the charity. He called their headquarters to double-check. They hadn't received any money from Washington High.

The student assistant in the office overheard Mr. O'Connor talking to the principal and soon the whole school knew.

At first, Emily played the tearful victim of a terrible mistake. But the local newspaper did a full-scale investigation. They found that Emily's father had declared bankruptcy, and that the receipt Emily had given to Mr. O'Connor had a forged signature. The charity's accountant verified that no money had been received from Washington High, and the receipts from the stores where Emily had bought her new clothes added up to roughly the amount collected for the flood victims. News like that in their small town received front-page coverage.

Humiliated and desperate, Emily came to Jillian's house. "They can't take my grades away, so I'm still valedictorian," Emily sobbed. "But the salutatorian will give the graduation speech. The school says that someone charged with a crime isn't a good role model. I can't blame them. I never thought I was capable of stealing—but I'm guilty. What can I do now?"

"Do you remember when I said that salvation was God's free gift?" Jillian asked. Emily nodded. "When we humbly repent of our sins, ask Jesus for forgiveness, and are ready to surrender our lives to Him, we're eligible for eternal life. If you're interested in starting over again, I'll tell you more."

Emily was now ready to listen.

Although you may not be an unbeliever like Emily, you may be guilty of expecting God to fit into the framework of what makes sense to you. Even if you haven't decided that natural causes accounts for all living things, or that complex life forms evolved from simple life forms, you may be guilty of putting God in the box of your preference, your personality, or your desires.

ACTION STEPS TO RESIGNING FROM PLAYING GOD

1. Acknowledge that God is self-existent and independent, so He doesn't have to answer to anyone.
2. Remember that God's ways are higher and better than what you think is right.
3. Recognize that God makes all the rules, and they are fair, considered in the light of eternity.
4. Realize that salvation depends not upon human effort or intellect but upon God's provision.

WORDS TO LIVE BY

But the plans of the LORD stand firm forever,
    the purposes of his heart through all generations.

—Psalm 33:11

Our God is in heaven;
    he does whatever pleases him.

—Psalm 115:3

"For my thoughts are not your thoughts,
    neither are your ways my ways,"
    declares the LORD.
"As the heavens are higher than the earth,
    so are my ways higher than your ways
    and my thoughts than your thoughts."

—Isaiah 55:8–9

DON'T MISS OUT ON MIRACLES

DID YOU KNOW?

Fish don't sleep. They don't have eyelids.[1]

A horse can sleep standing up.[2]

Humans need an average of eight hours of sleep a night. (That means that most people who live to be age seventy-two have slept for a total of twenty-four years in their lifetimes!)

Cows get along just fine on three hours of sleep every twenty-four hours.

Giraffes sleep about ten minutes a day.

When dolphins sleep, half of their brains remain awake to keep them swimming![3]

Our world is filled with amazing phenomena that no one can fully explain.

Elephants, for instance, post their own guards, who raise their trunks if there's danger. Although a sentry elephant may be as far as one-and-a-half miles away, the rest of the herd goes on alert. Humans haven't a clue as to how this communication takes place.[4]

Even more mysterious is the case of the "talking trees." In 1983, two biologists placed swarms of predatory caterpillars on the branches of willow trees. The purpose was to find out how trees defend them-selves against attack. Within hours, the chemical composition of the leaves began to change, which caused them to taste terrible. The change also made their protein indigestible, which killed the predators. Unbelievably, nearby trees—whose roots and leaves weren't touching those that were being invaded by caterpillars—activated the same defense system.[5]

Another puzzle has to do with the sequoia. Water must travel up from the roots of the sequoia tree to the top branches, a distance of four hundred feet. How can a tree generate pressure of about 420 pounds per square inch to raise the water that high?[6]

Photosynthesis poses other questions for scientists. This process is so complicated, it's thought to involve as many as five hundred chemical steps, only a few of which are fully understood.[7] Yet even the simplest of plants perform this chemistry.

A further mystery involves the incredible energy and sense of direction of certain creatures. Every fall, for instance, the ruby-throated hummingbird flies five hundred miles, nonstop, across the Gulf of Mexico—and makes the return trip the following spring. Metabolic tests suggest that the bird, which weighs one-tenth of an ounce, is too small to store up enough energy for the task. But the hummingbird, of course, doesn't know that![8]

Many species of butterflies travel up to six hundred miles nonstop. With the wind behind them, some have flown across the Atlantic Ocean.[9] Monarch butterflies travel over two thousand miles to winter in the precise location where their ancestors did.[10]

The Arctic tern makes the longest known migratory trip from the Arctic to Antarctica—a distance of 22,000 miles each year. A tern banded in England on July 25, 1982, was caught 11,000 miles away in Melbourne, Australia—just 115 days later. It had flown an average of almost 100 miles a day.[11]

Equally baffling is the salmon. When it's time for a salmon to lay its eggs, it returns to the exact area of the riverbed where it was spawned four years earlier. Although it has spent most of those four years in the ocean, it knows where it needs to go and what it has to do. It will even leap fifteen feet up the sides of waterfalls to get there.[12]

All of these remarkable examples suggest that the Creator of the universe is a lot smarter and more powerful than all humans com-

bined. Knowing that God has total wisdom, knowledge, and strength
has some wonderful implications for our lives.

DOES IT MATTER?

For Evan, mountain climbing had become a passion. He'd taken several classes, learned the correct techniques, acquired the right equipment,
and had participated in several climbs. Now, because Evan had just completed the advanced mountaineering course, he and two classmates were
invited by their instructor, Mr. Kelly, to join him with some other experienced climbers on a week-long trip. Their goal was to reach a high peak
that had a fantastic view. Since both the trip and Evan's eighteenth birthday fell during spring break, he convinced his parents to let him go.

As they were airlifted to their base camp, they commented on the
perfect weather and the favorable forecast. But Mr. Kelly, the veteran
Alaskan mountaineer, made them listen once more to the emergency
information.

"With perfect conditions," he explained, "we'll be home by evening
of the fourth day. But we've planned a few extra days in case of bad
weather."

They set up their base camp and tried to get a good night's sleep.
Rising early, they hoped to make good time—and their first day was
very successful. By 10:00 a.m. on the third day, they had neared the
twin peaks of the summit. The first peak looked like a giant wave of
frosting, and behind it stood the more cone-shaped peak, which was
their goal.

Even at their current altitude, the view was impressive. Evan couldn't
wait to get to the top. But in order to cross a series of deep crevasses,
the instructor, along with the other expert climbers, took three less
experienced climbers across first while Evan, Josh, and Lander waited
their turn.

Suddenly, they heard a loud crack, followed by a thundering roar.
The earth quaked, snow flew everywhere, and the three boys were
tobogganed downhill, shaken and tumbled as if they were on a tilt-a-
whirl without being strapped in.

When the commotion was over, Evan spotted Lander, and within five minutes, they had located Josh—but only Evan still had his backpack. They had just survived an avalanche! The snowscape had changed drastically and they were now at the edge of an icy cliff. A few yards away, the first crevasse their friends had traversed had lengthened and widened into an uncrossable chasm. They were trapped—completely cut off from the outside world with no way of reaching their companions.

VITAL INFORMATION

Most people say they believe that God knows everything and can do anything. True Christians believe that Jesus Christ is God in human form. The wisdom of the words of Jesus, His ability to know what people are thinking, His great miracles, and His resurrection from the dead show us what God is like. The Bible, God's revelation to humans, is full of events in which the miraculous power and knowledge of God is evident.

Too often we limit God to what *we* think He might be capable of doing. We see no way out, so we give up. We have no solution, so we muddle along, settling for second-rate living.

More believing prayer like that of Jeremiah, an Old Testament prophet, would greatly improve each day: "Sovereign LORD, you have made the heavens and the earth by your great power and outstretched arm. Nothing is too hard for you" (Jer. 32:17).

Decide to believe God and count on the supernatural. God's miracle could be to change the situation or it might be to transform you so that you experience victory in spite of difficult circumstances. Faith in the God of the impossible will radically improve your quality of life.

IF EVAN PUTS HIS FAITH IN THE GOD OF MIRACLES, HIS STORY COULD HAVE A HAPPY ENDING . . .

They stood there in silence, staring around them, completely overwhelmed. The thought came to Evan, *If there was ever a time to put my faith in an all-powerful God into practice, it's now.*

"Guys," he said, "let's pray." He led them in the most fervent prayer he'd ever prayed.

In the silence after their prayer, Mr. Kelly's words came back to them: "Conserve your energy and use your small, lightweight shovels to hollow out a snow shelter."

Using Evan's shovel, they took turns digging out a snow cave. Then, finding a patch of smooth snow, they stamped out the word *HELP*. They hoped that a pilot might see it.

As they tried to figure out what else they could do, Evan remembered the red silk banner. His little sister had won it in the solo contest, and he'd stuffed it into his jacket, hoping to be photographed with it on the mountain top. He'd planned to give an enlarged picture to his sister as a surprise. He took it out and spread it on the snow, weighing it down with some gear from his backpack. He hoped that it might be visible from the air. Now that they had done everything they could, there was nothing to do but sit and wait.

Lander maintained an outward cool, but soon Josh was nearly freaking out. Evan tried to comfort him and began to explain the plan of salvation to both of them. They listened and eagerly asked God to forgive their sins and invited Jesus into their hearts. Then the three of them prayed silently. At 3:30 in the afternoon, they ate the candy bars they had in their jackets.

When evening fell, the light of the full moon on the snow was breathtakingly beautiful, but the night seemed cruel and endless. Trying to keep warm, they huddled in their snow shelter. But by 3:00 a.m., cold, exhaustion, and hopelessness were threatening them like tangible enemies. It was tempting to just give up and go to sleep forever in the snow.

Evan thought he heard the sound of an engine, but emerging from their cold cave, the empty sky seemed to mock him. Feeling discouraged, he desperately prayed for strength, stamina—and a miracle.

Little did Evan know that a miracle was in the making. Monte, a commercial pilot was flying a special order to a construction company that wanted to complete a project before the deadline. Monte was ahead of schedule, so when he saw what looked like evidence of an avalanche, he lowered his altitude and, out of curiosity, made a fly-over. A dark square on the white snow caught his attention. Gazing intently on the scene below, he saw HELP spelled out in the snow. He immediately radioed air rescue, giving his exact location and telling what he saw.

Unaware of God's intervention and intensely conscious of his hunger pangs, Evan kept thinking about the food in his backpack. Why not offer to stay awake while his companions got some sleep—then he could eat it all? He seriously considered the idea—until a Sunday school picture flashed into his mind—Jesus being tempted by the Devil to turn stones into bread.

"Lord," he prayed silently, "I'm so sorry." As he shared the little he had, the three of them decided to let one person at a time sleep—and to do as much praying as possible.

At ten o'clock, the boys heard a thumping vibrating sound, and were overjoyed to see a helicopter descending to rescue them. Later, the whole story came together. The others had been lost in the avalanche. The commercial pilot had never crossed that area at night, and minutes after he'd taken off from the airport, the head contractor had called to cancel the flight. He'd be able to buy the necessary materials from a project that had been postponed, but since, by contract, he'd have to pay the pilot for use of the plane, he'd let the order stand.

Even the newspaper article about their rescue called it miraculous.

Before this experience, Evan had read about the Israelites at the Red Sea, David and Goliath, and Daniel in the lions' den. He'd never known whether or not to take those stories literally, but now he believed every word—and was terribly grateful when he realized that "Evan and the avalanche" had been added to the list of God's miraculous deeds.

Phenomena abound in nature that the most knowledgeable scientists can't explain, and things that defy human understanding continue to occur. Why not put your faith in a supernatural God and get in on the miracles God wants to perform for you?

ACTION STEPS TOWARD EXPECT-A-MIRACLE LIVING

1. Whenever a crisis hits, build your faith by reading about some of God's great deliverance of people in the past. Look at the following for starters:
   - Exodus 14:1–31—Red Sea Wonder
   - 2 Chronicles 20:1–30—Praise Plasters Enemy
   - Daniel 3:1–30—Fiery Furnace Facts
   - Daniel 6:1–28—Angel Induced Lion Lockjaw
   - Acts 16:16–40—Earthquaked to Freedom
   - Acts 27:13–44—Don't Give Up the Ship Until You See the Shore
2. Confess any pride or other sin to God. Study the following passages to know how to pray: 2 Chronicles 7:14 and Psalm 66:16–20.
3. Remember that God answers believing prayer. See Philippians 4:6–7; James 5:16; and 1 John 5:14–15.
4. Trust that God will take care of you, and rest in His love. Look at Isaiah 26:3; John 14:27; and 1 Peter 5:7 to see where God promises to do that for us.

WORDS TO LIVE BY

Do you know how the clouds hang poised,
   those wonders of him who is perfect in knowledge?
                                        —Job 37:16

For you are great and do marvelous deeds;
   you alone are God.
                                        —Psalm 86:10

Great is our Lord and mighty in power;
   his understanding has no limit.
                                        —Psalm 147:5

YOUR LIFE HAS A SPECIAL PURPOSE

DID YOU KNOW?

The odds against life spontaneously forming on Earth are beyond imagination.

Sir Fred Hoyle, British scientist, mathematician, and astronomer, calculated the possibility statistics on just one single cell developing anywhere in the universe. The chances that all the functional proteins necessary for life might form in one place by random events, he discovered, are one chance in 10^{40}, that is one chance in 10,000,000,000,000,000,000,000,000,000,000,000,000,000.[1]

To help you understand odds like 1 in 10^{40}, here are some other statistics for comparison:

- Your chance of winning a really big lottery twice in a row is 1 in 100,000 billion—that's only 10^{14} or 100,000,000,000,000.[2]
- It would take only 10^{17} (100,000,000,000,000,000) silver dollars to cover the entire state of Texas two feet deep.[3]
- The number of snowflakes that have fallen on planet Earth since the beginning of time is only 10^{35} (100,000,000,000,000,000,000,000,000,000,000,000).[4]

It's easy to see why Sir Fred Hoyle's discovery was such big news. To give you even more of an idea of the impossibility of those chances, consider—if a billion continents, each the size of North America, were totally covered with stacks of dimes that were 239,000 miles high (the distance between the Earth and the moon), the possibility that a blind-folded person could pick out the one dime that had been painted red *on the first try* would be roughly equivalent to 1 in 10^{40}.[5]

"From a practical standpoint, scientists have determined that any-thing beyond one chance in 10^{50} is beyond reason . . . essentially im-possible or absurd. (Like someone correctly picking the lottery seven times in a row)."[6]

The odds, then, of macroevolution changing a single cell ameba into a reptile . . . that became a bird . . . that produced a land mammal . . . who gave birth to an ape . . . that evolved into a human are "FAR LESS LIKELY than winning thousands of lotteries in a row. Statisti-cally, evolution is 'impossible.'"[7]

But, as Dr. Hoyle has shown, it would also be impossible to pro-duce even the first cell. Since billions of cells would need to be as-sembled, Hoyle—although he was not previously religious—decided that there must be a God. That life could result from time, chance, and the properties of matter, Hoyle concluded, is roughly equivalent to believing that "a tornado sweeping through a junk yard might as-semble a Boeing 747 from the materials therein."[8]

Other probability calculations are even more pessimistic. "Molecular biophysicist Harold Horowitz calculated that if one were to take the simplest living cell and break every chemical bond within it, the odds that the cell would reassemble under ideal natural conditions would be one chance in $10^{100,000,000,000}$."[9]

Carl Sagan and Francis Crick, two outspoken evolutionists, tried to make the case that life came to us from another universe in outer space. They estimated that the difficulty of evolving a human by chance pro-cesses alone would be one chance in $10^{2,000,000,000}$.[10] And it seems that these very important scientists forgot something—this evolved hu-man would need someone to marry if the race were to continue!

Since random chance can't put together the ingredients for even one cell, it's evident that the great Designer invented the cell and is behind the blueprint for life itself. God allowed you to be born be-cause He wanted to love you—just the way you are. He has a special plan for your life—and that of each human—a plan no one else is uniquely fitted to accomplish.

You can say with David, "The LORD will fulfill his purpose for me" (Ps. 138:8). And when things get tough you can pray the rest of that verse with him: "Your love, O LORD, endures forever—do not abandon the works of your hands." God will hear you petition and He will take care of you.

DOES IT MATTER?

Scott just couldn't shake the depression that engulfed him. He'd been born to a single mom, who told him that his father was a very nice man and that she had loved him deeply. But things just didn't work out for the wedding they'd planned.

Scott's stepfather showed favoritism to his own children, making Scott feel left out and frustrated. But the bombshell came when he'd eavesdropped on his mother's conversation with his aunt.

He'd left the house to play in a baseball game, but when the umpire failed to appear, the coaches postponed the game and sent their players home. Unaware of his presence in the kitchen, his mother and aunt were talking out on the deck. "Sandy," his aunt argued, "how can *you* judge Melissa. If it hadn't been for your car accident on the way to the abortion clinic, Scott wouldn't be here today."

"I know," Scott's mother had replied, "but what would *you* have done? The man who got me pregnant was married, was a drug dealer, and he'd been lying to me about *everything*."

The thought that his mother never really wanted him was more than Scott could take. In school, he'd been taught that all things came into existence through random chance. Now he decided he was an accident—in more ways than one—and that there really was no reason to go on living.

VITAL INFORMATION

What comfort is there for Scott when he wonders about the purpose of his life? What comfort is there for you? God says to you, "I have loved you with an everlasting love; I have drawn you with lov-ing-kindness" (Jer. 31:3). His love is unconditional, and whether you respond to that love or not, God cares about you.

He made you with a special purpose in mind. No matter the cir-cumstances of your birth, the situation in your family, or the frustra-tions you must overcome, God is at work to cut through the sin, the insensitivity, the prejudice, and the mistakes of others in order to bless you and use you.

IF SCOTT PAYS ATTENTION TO WHAT GOD HAS TO SHOW HIM, THE CONTINUATION OF HIS STORY COULD GO LIKE THIS . . .

Scott even thought of taking his own life. But to his great surprise a special speaker addressed his youth group on the subject of suicide.

"I'd venture to say," he began, "that several of you in this room have probably thought of suicide. There's something you need to know. Those thoughts of ending your life come straight from Satan himself. The Devil is a robber, and he's described in John 10:10 as a thief, who comes only to steal and kill and destroy. You must learn to reject those thoughts of self destruction.

"Deuteronomy 32:39 says, 'There is no god besides me. . . . I bring to life.' Your life—even if your parents didn't want you—was espe-cially created by God for a special purpose that no one else can fill. God loves you more than any human father ever could. You are of infinite value because He created you as a designer original."

Scott was shocked. It was as if God were speaking directly to him. The speaker continued. "God is making the greatest power in the world available to you tonight. It's the ability to forgive your enemies, to forgive people who have hurt you, even if those people happen to be your parents. God can replace hate and resentment with the ability to love. Your willingness to forgive is the container into which He can pour that power to forgive."

The speaker asked those who had contemplated suicide and those who needed to forgive someone to come forward. Scott joined the others. Jed, the college guy who came to talk with him, was so nice that Scott ended up telling him everything. It felt good to talk it out.

Jed assured Scott of God's great love for him. "Every time you doubt God's love for you," Jed suggested, "read about the crucifixion of Jesus. Remember, if you'd been the only person in the world, Jesus would have died just for you."

When Scott said he was willing to forgive his real father, his stepfather, and his mother, Jed led him in a prayer, asking God for the power to forgive. He advised Scott that each time the resentment tried to return, he should pray, "God, I'm willing to forgive. Give me the power I need."

"And every time the thought comes into your mind that you're an accident," Jed told Scott, "reject the idea. Instead, quote Jeremiah 1:5: 'Before I formed you in the womb I knew you.'"

Jed also told Scott to make an appointment with the youth pastor whenever he was discouraged and really needed to talk to someone.

Although he had his ups and downs, Scott did try to put Jed's advice into practice. Scott got a concordance and looked up every verse on the love of God that he could find. He wrote them down in a notebook to read when he felt discouraged.

The next time his stepfather planned something for his younger brothers without including him, Scott prayed, "I'm willing to forgive. Please give me Your power." Scott continued to reject the idea that he was an accident, and found that talking periodically with his youth pastor gave him strategies for dealing with his problems.

When Scott's friend Dale was having trouble getting along with his stepfather, Scott was able to pass along some useful advice. He told Dale that knowing Jesus had given him the power to love his stepfather—and Dale could see that he really meant it. Dale even started to attend youth group with Scott. The day that Dale accepted Christ as his Savior made Scott realize the very special purpose that God had for Scott's life. It had been the Lord's plan to use a person with similar problems to reach out to Dale—and Scott had been that person.

Remember, the odds that even one cell could come together

by accident are one in 10,000,000,000,000,000,000,000,000,000, 000,000,000,000,000. It's obvious, then, that God put a lot of thought into designing you. There's no one just like you in the universe. Your Maker loves and appreciates you, His special creation. Spend some time reflecting on this when you feel down.

STEPS FOR CONQUERING THE I-FEEL-UNLOVED-AND-UNWANTED SYNDROME

1. Read the following Bible verses about God's love for you and make them a part of your life:
   - Psalms 57:9–10; 103:11–14; 107:1
   - John 15:9–10, 13–14
   - 1 John 4:9–10, 18–19
2. Read about the crucifixion of Jesus in Matthew 26:36–27:54, remembering that He suffered all that because He loves you.
3. Realize that God carefully planned your life. You are not an accident.
4. Each time someone hurts you, pray, "I'm willing to forgive, Lord. Give me the power I need."
5. Find a mature Christian friend who will guard your secrets and give you godly advice.

WORDS TO LIVE BY

The LORD will fulfill his purpose for me;
   your love, O LORD, endures forever.
                                        —Psalm 138:8

For you created my inmost being;
   you knit me together in my mother's womb.
I praise you because I am fearfully and wonderfully
      made …
   I know that full well …
All the days ordained for me

were written in your book
before one of them came to be.

—Psalm 139:13–14, 16

As you do not know the path of the wind,
   or how the body is formed in a mother's womb,
so you cannot understand the work of God,
   the Maker of all things.

—Ecclesiastes 11:5

21

BEATING BOREDOM

The wonders of water go well beyond its satisfying your thirst on a hot day. But just in case you're interested, you're likely to guzzle down 16,000 gallons of water in your lifetime.

Water also gives you a place to swim and makes it possible for plants to grow. Many things that you see are made up mostly of water. An elephant and an ear of corn are about seventy percent water, while a potato and an earthworm are about eighty percent water.

Water is the only substance on Earth that's naturally present as not only a liquid, but as a solid and a gas.[1] And in these three forms, water does some pretty amazing things in ways that are not always obvious. Water in the form of ice, for instance, breaks up rocks and produces soil. Water in the form of snow and rain moistens and cleanses the earth. In its vapor state, water condenses to form dew, which provides extra humidity for plant life over large areas.

As a solvent, water dissolves almost everything in the world[2]—sand and oil being among the exceptions.[3] Watery solutions help dissolve what living things eat and carry it to all parts of the organism.[4] When you think about it, it's pretty incredible that water is able to dissolve everything necessary for life's processes without dissolving the body organs or the organic substances that facilitate the processes.[5]

Water is present, too, in the clouds. The water-vapor level in our atmosphere is, in fact, perfect for providing enough rainfall so that advanced life can exist on the Earth.[6] If the clouds surrounding Earth were like the clouds around Venus, nothing could grow.

But water has even more unique properties that contribute to its value for life on Earth. Unlike almost every other liquid, water expands and weighs less when frozen. If it didn't, lakes and rivers would freeze from the bottom up.[7] "If ice sank, the Earth would become a lifeless arctic desert. Each winter, more and more ice would pile up on the bottom of lakes, rivers, and oceans. In summer, the sun's heat could not reach deeply enough to melt the ice. Water life would die. The hydrologic cycle [which controls rain and water evaporation] would slow down. In time, all of the water would turn to solid ice, except for a thin layer of water over ice in summer."[8]

It's interesting, too, that the internal structure of a molecule of water is just right to regulate the Earth's temperature, making it favorable for life. If the electric polarity—the amount of separation between the positive and negative poles within the water molecule—were greater, so much heat would be generated during the formation of ice and the condensation of water vapor into raindrops that people couldn't live on the planet. But if the electric polarity within the water molecule were smaller, water could not be the solvent that is necessary for life chemistry to proceed.[9]

Besides the life-giving properties of water, it also provides ways to have fun. In addition to the obvious recreational value of water sports, water in the form of snow provides opportunities for winter sports like skiing, skating, and snowboarding. The existing properties of the water molecule combined with atmospheric conditions produce snow, as well as snowflake patterns. The shape of the snowflake depends upon the temperature. Six-sided plates form only if the temperature is at or below the freezing point (32 degrees Fahrenheit or 0 degrees centigrade). In colder weather, snow takes the form of needles or hollow prisms.[10]

Snowflakes form without any external information or programming, and are thus being formed "naturally." For that reason, it has been suggested that snowflakes support the evolutionary theory that living organisms appeared spontaneously. But snowflakes, unlike living organisms, do not have information-rich genetic codes that determine their development. Nor do they do possess the ability to reproduce.[11]

Australian microbiologist Michael Denton observes that the difference between a living cell and a snowflake "is a chasm as vast and absolute as it is possible to conceive."[12]

Just as God provides water for a variety of processes that make life possible—and enjoyable—He makes spiritual resources available to us. Experiencing the Spirit of God can, in fact, give us love, joy, peace, and all the good stuff for which everybody is looking. It's no wonder that His gifts for the soul are often compared to water.

DOES IT MATTER?

Casey had a bad case of "the blahs." He wasn't quite sure what the problem was.

Sure, his parents fought a lot, but what else was new?

He didn't like school, but that had been going on since the fourth grade.

He wasn't very popular with the girls, and his basketball team was losing a lot of games, but both were a repeat of last year.

There wasn't anything exciting to do in his small town, but he'd never expected there would be. His grandfather talked about the big parade in 1968 when a presidential candidate paid a visit. That was probably the most exciting thing that had ever happened in their town.

No, nothing had changed since last year. But this year, for some reason, Casey felt like a robot. Every morning, he got out of bed (after his mother yelled a few times). He showered, dressed, and grabbed a couple of doughnuts for breakfast. Then he sat through all his classes, went to basketball practice, ate dinner, did some homework, watched TV, and finally hit the sack—in order to repeat the process the next day. Something was missing, but Casey couldn't figure out what it was.

VITAL INFORMATION

How can Casey—or you—fill up the hollowness you feel inside? Jesus answered that question when He said, "If anyone is thirsty, let him come to me and drink. Whoever believes in me, as the Scripture has said, streams of living water will flow from within him" (John 7:37–38). The apostle John explains, "By this he meant the Spirit, whom those who believed in him were later to receive" (John 7:39). God, through the Holy Spirit, is the source of all you need.

IF CASEY SEEKS GOD'S SOLUTION FOR HIS PROBLEM, HIS STORY MIGHT CONTINUE LIKE THIS . . .

Casey consoled himself with the thought that no one had ever died of boredom. Yet he knew something was wrong. Wasn't a real Christian supposed to be excited about life?

He remembered the day he gave his life to Christ. He was only twelve. Watching the *Jesus* movie at his church made Casey see for the first time that Jesus died for his sins. He felt guilty and dirty and wanted to be clean. He realized how much Jesus had suffered for him and wanted to give his whole life to the Lord.

After going forward to make a public confession of his faith, verbalizing his plea for forgiveness, and telling God to make all the changes necessary in his life, he never doubted his salvation. But he felt like he was missing something.

As Casey prayed about his lackluster existence, a plan formed in his mind. Maybe he could talk to someone, but who? Someone he knew, a person who felt comfortable talking about faith and about God. Of course! Casey knew someone like that, someone who always had a smile and an encouraging word. Mr. Brandt! He must know the secret.

Mr. Brandt got around on crutches. He had lost a leg in the Vietnam War, and skin problems prevented him from wearing a prosthetic leg. When his wife died, people predicted that he'd lose his optimistic attitude. But it didn't happen. He always had a smile on his face and enjoyed spending time with the kids at church.

There was no basketball practice the day before Thanksgiving, so Casey made his way to Mr. Brandt's house after school. Mr. Brandt greeted him at the door, and the two exchanged small talk for a few minutes. But soon, Mr. Brandt's friendly way of listening made it easy for Casey to explain everything that was on his heart. Mr. Brandt listened carefully before saying anything.

"Many years ago," he began, "a miner was hopelessly lost in the desert. He was weak and dizzy from lack of food and water. Just when all hope was gone, he stumbled onto a wide rushing river with a big waterfall. Content that his life had been spared, he built a makeshift hut, fashioned a fishing pole, and existed on the fish he caught and the wild berries he found. Do you think he acted wisely?"

Casey's brow furrowed and he blinked a few times. "Well . . . I guess that way of living would be okay . . . for a while. But after he regained his strength, he could have gone down the river and found other people. Maybe he could have come back and built a settlement on the river . . . used the water to change the desert . . . irrigate crops." Casey was warming to the idea by now. "They could use the falls for hydroelectric power and maybe build a manufacturing plant." The principle of the story at last dawned on Casey—and he put it into words. "He missed a lot of opportunities to make money and better his life."

"Forgive me for saying so, Casey," Mr. Brandt said gently, "but you're a lot like that miner. He used the water to save his life, and he was content with that. You've depended on the Holy Spirit to save your soul, but how about plugging into His supernatural power? You could show the love of Jesus to people in practical ways, witness to your friends at school. You could read your Bible every day to find out what God wants you to do. You could organize your friends and do something worthwhile, maybe sponsor Christian concerts and other evangelistic events. I'll bet there are other teens in town who are bored. Receiving God's love in order to give it away puts a spark into any life.

"I learned a long time ago," Mr. Brandt continued, "not to let circumstances form my prison. I consciously remember that Jesus is always by my side, and I talk to Him every few minutes by sending up a prayer, so I never go anywhere alone. When sadness or discouragement knock on my door, I just say, 'Jesus, what do I do now?'—and the answer is usually, 'Come up with some way to help another person.'"

Casey thanked Mr. Brandt and went straight to Jim's house. Jim was president of their church youth group. Casey knew that the two of them could organize some fun activities for the kids in their town, and after each event a short evangelistic talk could be given. He knew their youth pastor would help out.

Hillary had talked about the kids from the youth groups going to the retirement center to spend time with her grandmother and the other residents—especially the ones who didn't get many visitors. The young people could put on some programs—sing some worship songs, do a puppet presentation—and talk with the people afterwards. He and Jim could get something like that organized.

And the person in charge of working with the children at their church was always glad to have teens come by to help in their programs.

Suddenly, Casey had lots of ideas about things he and the other kids from his church could do to minister to others.

Like Casey, you can decide to reach out to others as you depend upon the Lord for all that you need. The God who invented water with all its incredible qualities stands ready to give the living water of His Holy Spirit to put spark and meaning into ordinary days and boring routine. It's up to you to turn on the faucet by praying and thirsting for more of God.

ACTION STEPS FOR BEATING BOREDOM

1. List ten things you could do to show God's love to other people—and begin to carry them out one by one, checking them off your list.

2. Learn how to clearly present the gospel, and trust the Holy Spirit for the boldness to share it. Make a list of your friends who don't know Jesus and pray for them. Receive from the Holy Spirit instructions and power for finding ways to share the gospel with them. You might, for instance, invite a friend to your house to see a Christian video. You could invite another to an event at your church. Give your intellectual classmate something to read that will challenge him or her to think about Jesus.

3. Don't just read the Bible; put it into practice.
4. Think of Jesus as being physically beside you all the time and learn to talk over with Him each detail of your life.

WORDS TO LIVE BY

I am the vine; you are the branches. If a man remains in me and I in him, he will bear much fruit; apart from me you can do nothing.

—John 15:5

Continue to work out your salvation with fear and trembling, for it is God who works in you to will and to act according to his good purpose.

—Philippians 2:12–13

22

WEAPONS FOR WINNING

Animals—and even plants—are equipped to protect themselves.

Monarch butterflies, for example, feed on poisonous milkweed while in their caterpillar state. The toxins remain in the body of the adult butterfly, making them taste so bitter and disagreeable that birds usually won't eat them.[1] The viceroy butterfly, on the other hand, tastes just fine, but it stays out of birds' beaks because its appearance is similar to the monarch butterfly.[2]

Other kinds of insects also have methods of self-defense. A bombardier beetle, when attacked by a toad, shoots a stream of boiling noxious gas that coats the toad's outstretched tongue with a bad-tasting film.[3] Some millipedes defend themselves by using clouds of lethal hydrogen cyanide gas. Released through vents in their sides, the poison can be aimed at the attacker.

At least one African species of millipede can fire broadsides in two directions at the same time—like a battleship on legs.[4] Tropical termites send jets of quick-setting glue from an apparatus in their heads. The stickiness of the glue immobilizes marauding ants while its smell calls other termite soldiers to the battle.[5]

Ingenious weaponry is found in higher forms of animals as well. The "glass snake" lizard is able to break off its tail at the halfway point. The dismembered tail, still sometimes wiggling, serves as a decoy while the real lizard scurries for safety—and waits for a shorter tail to grow back.[6]

The frill of the Australian frilled lizard normally lies flat along its neck. But when the lizard is in full defense mode, it lifts the frill, which stands out in a disk and can measure up to two feet across. In this defense posture, hissing loudly, the three-foot lizard appears quite formidable, but is in reality rather harmless.[7]

The Eastern hog nose snake, when in danger, simply plays dead.[8]

Lobsters survive by teamwork. When lobsters in the Bahamas migrate to deeper water, each lobster hooks one pair of its front legs around the crustacean ahead, or flicks its antennae to maintain contact. (Sometimes, these "parades" can be up to fifty lobsters long.) In this way, each lobster's vulnerable belly and tail is protected by the armored legs and antennae of the one behind as they scuttle across the ocean floor.[9]

Another sea creature with powerful self-defense is the electric eel of South America. It has enough voltage in its tail to light a dozen household bulbs or to kill a man on contact.[10]

Blue whales, it seems, possess an alarm system. They have been known to emit whistles louder than a jet plane. In one case, the moan of five whales seems to have been picked up by another whale more than 100 miles away.[11]

Birds, too, are not without resources. The woodcock, for example, has a 360-degree range of vision, enabling it to see both in front and in back.[12]

Land mammals also use various methods to protect themselves. Foxes use speed and intelligence to outmaneuver their enemies, often wearing them down by running in circles and leading them on a wild goose chase. The red fox stays well ahead of its pursuer, reaching speeds of up to twenty-six miles per hour.[13]

A skunk can accurately spray an opponent in the eye from a distance of thirteen to sixteen feet. The putrid yellow liquid causes hours of discomfort and can cause temporary blindness.[14]

Badgers, as masters of the disappearing act, can dig themselves out of sight in ten minutes.[15]

Even plants protect themselves. A desert brittle bush drops poisonous leaves, killing off seedlings of other plants that could grow up to threaten its water supply.[16]

It's a no-brainer that Someone extremely intelligent put all these ingenious defense systems into place. It's comforting to know that the God who cares for all He has made has protection plans to keep you safe from your enemy, the Devil. It might be smart to find out what those protections are.

DOES IT MATTER?

It was the evening of Carly's birthday party. Her parents had reserved a private room at an Italian restaurant—the one that had the best pizza in town.

Brianna carefully wrapped the gift she'd bought and dressed for the occasion. Viewing herself in the full-length mirror, though, she was overcome with anguish. She felt fat and ugly. And pizza was her favorite food.

She'd promised herself a hundred times that she'd never vomit up her food again or take laxatives. And a hundred times she'd vowed to stay on a diet and start exercising—tomorrow.

As Brianna entered the restaurant, she put on her life-of-the-party mask, telling jokes that made everyone laugh. During the party, she pigged out on pizza, ending her meal with a huge, hot-fudge sundae.

Minutes later, Brianna felt that irresistible urge—like an unseen presence—driving her to the bathroom to vomit up her food. Brianna didn't realize, though, that she was not alone. That night, Carly's suspicions about her friend were confirmed.

VITAL INFORMATION

God could kill the Devil if He wanted to. He could have chosen to give you a life with no obstacles, no challenges—and no victories. But rather than make life easy, the Lord designed each day so that it cannot be lived well without His assistance. If you continually depend upon Him, you'll develop an intimate relationship with the Creator of the universe.

His Word contains the winning strategy: "Submit yourselves, then, to God. Resist the devil, and he will flee from you" (James 4:7). God wants you to experience the joy of being a winner.

IF BRIANNA'S OPEN TO GOD, SHE COULD EXPERIENCE HIS POWER TO OVERCOME . . .

Carly prayed about the best way to confront Brianna and about what she could do to help her. Finally, she confided in her youth pastor.

Taking the initiative, Pastor John invited the girls to his office. The atmosphere was tense as Carly explained her suspicions that Brianna suffered from bulimia. All the while, Carly affirmed her friendship and desire to help.

Brianna cried as she admitted to everything.

Pastor John reassured Brianna. He told both girls that the Devil had no power to create and that his only tool was deception. Using the white board behind his desk, Pastor John outlined Satan's strategy to destroy people.

1. Satan makes you believe a big lie—in this case that being extra thin is the most important thing in life.
2. The Devil convinces you that God can't or won't help you with the problem.
3. The Devil or his demons put thoughts and impulses in your mind, convincing you that they originated in your own head.
4. The enemy tries to conceal that you have power in Christ to resist these thoughts and urges.

Pastor John summed up the strategy for plugging into supernatural power: "It's basically prayer, following biblical principles, engaging in spiritual warfare, and obeying God. But so you get some precise pointers for your specific problem," said Pastor John, handing Brianna a business card, "I'd like you to see this Christian counselor."

Brianna started reading her Bible and praying every day. When she felt the impulse to vomit, she made a stand in prayer, often calling Carly on the telephone so they could pray together.

Brianna also came to accept that she wasn't built to be super slender, and she started appreciating the way God had made her. She kept her appointments with the counselor and learned helpful information.

Slowly, she changed her eating habits and started swimming four times a week. Finally, the day came when she could fit into the next size smaller dress—without purging herself. Knowing that she was winning the battle by depending upon God was a great feeling.

Ever since sin entered this world through the disobedience of Adam and Eve, God has promised to be our defender against Satan's attacks. Unlike the members of the animal kingdom, which have defense systems that are activated by instinct, we need to admit that we can't overcome by using our own ingenuity. We must be willing to receive our strategy, our strength, and our defensive weapons from the God who said, "My power is made perfect in weakness" (2 Cor. 12:9). If we depend upon the Lord, the joy of overcoming can be ours.

ACTION STEPS TO DEFEATING SATAN

1. Remember that you are a perfect you. Don't let the Devil convince you that God made a mistake when He designed your body, your personality, or your abilities. It's the Devil's lie that you must prove your worth by being extraordinarily good-looking, superintelligent, or able to do something better than anyone else. Once you believe the Devil's lies, he has set you up for an inferiority complex that can open the door to a lot of temptations.

2. Blow the Devil's cover by realizing that what God says is always true: "You . . . have overcome . . . because the one who is in you is greater than the one who is in the world" (1 John 4:4).

3. Obey God in everything because disobedience is the Devil's key to your heart.
4. Depend upon God to defend you. He is the same God who told Moses: "The LORD will fight for you" (Ex. 14:14)—and who promises to take care of you.

WORDS TO LIVE BY

No temptation has seized you except what is common to man. And God is faithful; he will not let you be tempted beyond what you can bear. But when you are tempted, he will also provide a way out so that you can stand up under it.

—1 Corinthians 10:13

The Lord knows how to rescue godly men [and women] from trials.

—2 Peter 2:9

INSULATION AGAINST FUTURE SHOCK

DID YOU KNOW?

The woodpecker is a marvel. This amazing bird's little body is equipped with a host of interdependent functions, none of which will serve its purpose unless all are working together.

"Woodslammer" might, in fact, be a better name for a woodpecker, because its beak strikes a tree with such tremendous force. Excellent nerve and muscle coordination must produce a perfect hit since a miss could wrench the cover off the woodpecker's brain. But the woodpecker is very accurate, and it is outfitted with a tough bill, a heavy-duty skull, and shock-absorbing tissue between its bill and skull. It should be obvious that the woodpecker was created— possessing simultaneously all of these traits. If not, it could not have survived.

Woodpeckers are perfectly equipped, then, to drill holes in trees. They do so to store acorns, but they also hunt bark beetles. When the beetles hear the pounding, they crawl farther down into their holes. But a woodpecker has a long, sticky tongue, which puts an end to the beetles' escape plans.[1]

In explaining how impossible it would have been for a woodpecker to evolve its characteristics one at a time, biologist Dr. Gary Parker says this about the woodpecker's tongue:

If a bird gets a long, sticky tongue just by chance, what's it going to do with it? Dangling out of the bill, the tongue gets bit or even stepped on. As the bird is flying over a twig, the tongue could wrap around the twig and hang the hapless "pre-woodpecker." The answer for the woodpecker is to slip its tongue into a muscular sheath that wraps around the skull *under* the scalp and inserts into the right nostril! That makes good sense (and good science) if you're planning ahead, but poses real problems if your faith is in time and chance, trial and error. (You don't get another trial if the error is fatal!)[2]

So we see that the woodpecker's tongue, as well as its skull, beak, and unbelievable accuracy when striking a tree trunk, were custom made for Mr. Woodpecker. Without every detail of this elaborate system working perfectly—something impossible to achieve by a series of slowly evolved mutations—the woodpecker could not hunt beetles to satisfy its hunger.[3]

God, who created the incredible design that assures the woodpecker a well-balanced diet of acorns and beetles, guarantees that not one little bird is forgotten. There's no need for you to worry, then, because—to paraphrase Luke—you are worth more than many woodpeckers (see Luke 12:7).

You can also be sure that God has equipped you to face a future that He already knows about. You can trust Him to give you what you need when you need it.

DOES IT MATTER?

Eric wondered what would happen to him. He'd never known his father and had no idea where he was. Eric and his mom had always lived with Grandpa Jack. Eric's mother was busy, striving for promotions in her high-paying job, so she was often out of town. But Grandpa Jack had always been there for Eric.

Grandpa Jack was patient and loving, disciplining Eric when he disobeyed, helping him with homework, and taking him fishing. It was Grandpa Jack who had led Eric to Christ, who sat with him in church, and who showed him by example how to live the Christian life. And since his retirement, Grandpa Jack had turned into a super chef.

When Eric first noticed that his grandfather was getting forgetful, he didn't think much of it. But when Grandpa Jack put the mail in the refrigerator and almost burned the house down by using the barbecue lighter fluid in the fireplace, Eric's mother made a doctor's appointment. The diagnosis of Alzheimer's disease seemed more than Eric could cope with. According to the doctor, the grandfather that Eric knew would slowly cease to exist. But Eric still needed him.

VITAL INFORMATION

How can Eric—or you—cope with an uncertain future?

God had enough foresight to equip the woodpecker with everything it needs to survive. God has looked ahead, and He has planned to supply you with what you need each time your life takes an unexpected turn.

God's track record is impressive. He provided bread from heaven for the Israelites when they wandered in the desert, as well as cloud cover by day, and a pillar of fire for light and warmth at night. He reprogrammed some ravens so they'd bring food to Elijah during a drought. He used a huge fish to gulp down Jonah and transport him to land. He sent an angel lion tamer to protect Daniel. And He earthquaked Paul and Silas right out of their prison chains.

The Lord hasn't changed. When you don't want to wake up to face the same problem another day, remember—although the difficulty will still be there, so will your God.

IF ERIC SEEKS GOD AND COOPERATES WITH HIM, HIS STORY MIGHT CONTINUE LIKE THIS . . .

Eric couldn't imagine life without his grandfather—and he didn't want to.

His mother was the family rebel—very smart and successful, but not at all interested in doing the will of God. Eric knew that his mother loved him, but he also knew that he'd been an unwanted child, and he sensed a certain amount of rejection. His mother was usually too busy to really listen, and she pressured him to be a success—even in areas where he didn't have much ability.

If his grandfather lost his mind, what would Eric do?

Eric decided to pray like he'd never prayed before. As he discussed his problem with the Lord, he realized that he needed outside help. Eric made an appointment with his pastor.

"Eric," Pastor Jim said gently, "your first need is someone to talk to. You'll become frustrated when your grandfather's mind doesn't function the way it used to. So please call me when you want advice or just need to talk. I'm on call twenty-four hours a day.

"You're also going to need other kinds of assistance. I'll put you in touch with the local chapter of the Alzheimer's Association. But there's a whole congregation of people in this church who are willing to help. Don't hesitate to call. And I want you to make a pact with me—together, we'll pray for your mother as well as your grandfather. I feel God will use your grandfather's illness to bring her back to Him. Every time you and I talk, we'll pray for her."

Eric felt a lot better as he left his pastor's office. He kept praying for Grandpa Jack and for his mother, and he visited his pastor often. After several months, his mother came back to the Lord, and slowly his communication with her improved. Watching his grandfather's decline, however, broke Eric's heart. But he kept praying for his mother, for Grandpa Jack, and for himself.

The day came when it wasn't safe for his grandfather to be left alone, and Grandpa Jack had to go live with Eric's aunt and uncle in another state. A sense of loneliness and loss overwhelmed Eric. He dreaded coming home to an empty house, and even the thought of staying alone while his mother traveled scared him.

He took his needs to God in prayer and told his pastor all about them. And God answered in a most amazing way. The pastor arranged for Eric to stay with a family from church whenever his mother was gone. The three little boys in that family became like the brothers Eric never had, and he enjoyed spending time with them.

For Eric, the fear of the future was beginning to fade. He started trusting his all-powerful, all-knowing, and all-loving heavenly Father to look out for him. You, too, can conquer your fear of the future. Don't you think that God—who carefully planned to assure the future of something so small as a woodpecker—will take care of you?

ACTION STEPS FOR FACING AN UNCERTAIN FUTURE

1. Pray about each need and each fear that you have, trusting that God will provide.
2. Find a caring Christian adult who is competent to give you good counsel and help. (If the first person you go to disappoints you, don't give up. Just keep on looking.)
3. Be open to God's supplying your needs in unexpected ways.
4. Meditate on these verses that tell of the greatness of God:
   - Jeremiah 32:27
   - Psalms 18:2–3; 46:1; 147:5

     As you realize how big God is and praise Him for His character, your problems will seem a lot smaller.
5. Ask God to show you His comfort and His love.

WORDS TO LIVE BY

"For I know the plans I have for you," declares the LORD, "plans to prosper you and not to harm you, plans to give you hope and a future."

—Jeremiah 29:11

In him we were also chosen, having been predestined according to the plan of him who works out everything in conformity with the purpose of his will.

—Ephesians 1:11

God has said, "Never will I leave you; never will I forsake you."

—Hebrews 13:5

24

FOREVER HOPE

Order does not naturally flow from chaos. If you ran a movie backward, you'd see a broken cup reassemble itself, but that never happens in real life. We can't keep things from wearing out or breaking or disintegrating. The same goes for people, plants, and animals. Living things age and eventually die.[1]

Hugh Ross, Ph.D., states that, according to the second law of thermodynamics, "as time proceeds, the universe becomes progressively more disordered, decayed, and run down."[2] Put in different terms, heat always flows by itself from warmer to cooler objects, and that energy tends to become less ordered as time goes on. In other words, heat naturally chills out, and order decays or turns to chaos. A bowl of hot soup turns cold when it sits on the table (and would spoil if you left it there for a week), your favorite T-shirt fades and the fabric becomes thin, your room—which you cleaned on Saturday—looks like a tornado hit by the time your grandmother visits.[3]

Scientific evidence also indicates that everything is going in the direction of disintegration. Instead of new life-forms evolving, for example, fewer and fewer organisms are surviving. "Of all known forms of animal life ever to inhabit the earth, only 10 percent still exist today,"[4] and the "estimated number of animal species that have become extinct since 1980: 100,000."[5]

"Estimates of the current rate of extinction vary from a low of 1 species per day to a high of 5 species per hour."[6]

> Decline and even extinction, not *evolution* is the rule when we compare fossil sea life with the sort of marine invertebrates we find living today. In fact, all major groups, except perhaps groups including clams and snails are represented by greater variety and more complex forms as fossils than today.[7]

It hardly makes sense that in the distant past, time and chance produced ever more complex living things, when today species become extinct instead of adapting to changed environments.

Dr. Ross sums it up like this: "No one example of significant self-generation or self-organization can be found in the entire realm of nature. In fact nature shows us just the opposite . . . Without causation nothing happens and without organization by an intelligent being, systems tend toward lower and lower levels of complexity."[8]

Today we agree that explosions, as well as works of art and construction projects, all need brains behind them. Is it reasonable to believe, then, that billions of years ago energy and matter became spontaneously organized, bringing order out of chaos, without any cause whatsoever?

Humans can't create something out of nothing. Energy and matter are actually two forms of the same thing, and the combined amount of both remains constant. Mass and energy cannot be created or destroyed by people. Humans can turn mass into energy and vice versa, but the total amount of these two substances stays the same. It's possible to make new forms of matter out of those that already exist, but humans must start with something.[9]

If energy, matter, and natural forces brought everything into existence, they should be able to save us from destruction. But that isn't the case. Scientists believe that the second law of thermodynamics will ultimately force the universe into a condition known as "heat death."[10]

Why would God create a perfect universe and let it end in a heat death? Why does He permit things to decay and disintegrate, and allow people to get old and die? Good questions. And the Bible gives us the answer.

God plans to create something even more fantastic in the future. Christ will return before this "heat death" occurs, and God will make "a new heaven and a new earth, the home of righteousness" (2 Peter 3:13) in which everything will maintain in a state of complete perfection.

Knowing that you can look forward to experiencing this new creation will help you face life.

DOES IT MATTER?

Nick lagged behind, following his parents and younger sisters into the funeral home. The entrance seemed eerie and much too silent. They were ushered into a large room on the left, where girls from his youth group stood in front of the casket, crying audibly. As Nick approached, he saw the still and lifeless form of Joel, the guy who'd been his best friend.

As Nick stood there, he remembered the moment he'd heard the news. Nick had been washing the family car, and his dad came out of the house, wearing an unfamiliar expression. Joel, Nick's dad told him, had been killed in a bus accident during a teen missions trip to Bolivia.

Nick never finished washing the car, and he'd been walking around in a daze ever since. It couldn't be true! How could such a thing happen? Why?

Joel had saved his money for over a year to participate in this evangelistic effort. Besides getting straight A's in his Spanish class, he'd spent extra hours studying to better communicate with the teens in Bolivia.

Nick felt anger rising within him. It wasn't fair! The best Christian in their youth group was dead at the age of seventeen. Why didn't God use His power to prevent the accident? Didn't God realize that Joel was planning to be a missionary and that He'd just lost one of His best recruits? Didn't God care that Nick had lost his best friend ever? Nick didn't know what he'd do without Joel.

VITAL INFORMATION

The Bible tells us, "The creation was subjected to frustration . . . in hope that the creation itself will be liberated from its bondage to decay and brought into the glorious freedom of the children of God. . . . we wait eagerly for . . . the redemption of our bodies" (Rom. 8:20–21, 23). God's ultimate plan is to give us new immortal bodies that will experience no pain. We will inhabit those bodies in a new universe that is free from frustration, decay, and death.

Aging, seeing things wear out, and losing people we love remind us that we're made for a better world. Although Joel would be missed, his death was not a tragedy from heaven's point of view. It only meant that Joel got to see Jesus and enjoy heaven long before his friends. And God has comfort for Nick, plus a call for him to consider eternal values.

IF NICK BRINGS HIS FEELINGS OF PAIN AND LOSS TO GOD IN ORDER TO RECEIVE HIS COMFORT, THIS COULD BE THE CONTINUATION OF THE STORY . . .

The church was packed and some people stood in the back. When the youth pastor stood up to give the sermon at Joel's funeral, Nick was too overwhelmed to really listen. But he did, at last, tune in.

"Our purpose in living is to take as many people to heaven with us as possible," Pastor Rick was saying. "Although the conversion of each individual is different, usually God uses several people to help a person see the need of salvation.

"A Christian presents the gospel to a friend, but the friend rejects the message. Another believer shows unusual Christian kindness to that friend. A third prays for the friend when he or she is facing problems. Yet another invites that friend to a Christian concert where he or she makes the decision to accept Christ.

"Joel lived out his concern to see others come to Jesus. Many of you will be in line to thank Joel once you reach heaven, because some of you will be there because Joel witnessed to you."

The pastor continued, "We mourn our loss. Tears will flow, and our hearts will ache. How good to know that the Lord is our comfort, that we can tell Jesus how we feel and let Him put His arms around us. It is right that we grieve, but I also call you to action. I'm asking every young person who is here today, are you willing to rededicate your life to the cause for which Joel gave his? If so, I invite you to come to the front."

Moved, Nick walked toward the platform with many others. With tears in his eyes, he told the Lord he'd do whatever was His will.

His resolve was, of course, tested. When school started in September, he missed Joel more than ever. He didn't know who to eat lunch with, and there was no one to greet him at his locker each morning. But he noticed things he'd never seen before—guys who seemed lonely, those with looks of sadness.

Although naturally shy, Nick approached a new kid. "Hi. How ya doin'?" he said with a sincere smile. "You're new, aren't you? My name's Nick."

"I'm Jacob," said the new kid, looking genuinely pleased at Nick's friendliness. "Glad to meet ya."

"Why don't we meet for lunch?" Nick suggested. "Maybe I can help you navigate through all the new-school stuff."

"Great," Jacob responded. "Thanks!"

"Sure thing," said Nick, already feeling better. "I'll wait for you by the pop machine."

And Jacob showed up. While they ate lunch, Nick learned that Jacob's parents had just divorced, and that he and his mom had moved to Springfield to live with his grandmother. As Jacob told his story, Nick could see the pain in his eyes. Because of the grief Nick was experiencing, he was now more sensitive to the needs of others.

Nick determined to start praying for Jacob, become his friend and, just like Joel would have done, look for an opportunity to share Jesus with him.

An awareness that this world isn't made to last indefinitely and a decision to invest your life in things of everlasting value will help Nick—and you—when times are tough. The eternal perspective will allow you to receive God's comfort when what is most important is taken from you. Take solace in this: Because you have Jesus, you have forever hope.

ACTION STEPS FOR DEALING WITH LOSS AND DISAPPOINTMENT

1. Set your sights on the things that last forever: the Word of God and the souls of those with whom you come in contact.
2. Tell God about the pain you feel, ask Him for His comfort, and let His Word speak to your heart.
3. Use the sensitivity that suffering gives you to reach out to others who are hurting.
4. Put things in the perspective of eternity. It might seem terribly dark right now, but this time of trouble is only a split second in comparison with eternity.

WORDS TO LIVE BY

Heaven and earth will pass away, but my words will never pass away.

—Matthew 24:35

Man is destined to die once, and after that to face judgment.

—Hebrews 9:27

Then I saw a new heaven and a new earth, for the first heaven and the first earth had passed away. ... And God himself will be with them and be their God. He will wipe every tear from their eyes. There will be no more death or mourning or crying or pain, for the old order of things has passed away.

—Revelation 21:1, 3–4

CUSTOM-MADE BY AN AWESOME CREATOR

DID YOU KNOW?

Animals come equipped with special survival gear.

The polar bear's coat, for example, is specifically designed for the cold. Made up of clear, hollow hairs, it traps ultraviolet light and conducts it to the bear's skin, where it is changed to heat. The fur insulates so well that it holds in 95 percent of the animal's warmth.[1]

Polar bears also have a way to get through long hibernation periods—they overeat. The average Alaskan male polar bear weighs 1,000 pounds and can lose 25 percent of his fat during hibernation. But because he stores up fat from large amounts of food, when he wakes up, he's still healthy.[2]

The emperor penguin, another cold weather animal, has thick and oily feathers, custom-made for its needs. The feathers form a waterproof coat that keeps the penguin dry no matter how long it stays in the icy waters of Antarctica. The white underside of a penguin helps it blend with the sunlit sky and water, making it hard for predators to see it if viewed from below. Seen from above, the penguin's dark back matches the blackness of the ocean depths.[3]

Another way these penguins (which stand about four feet high and can weigh up to one hundred pounds),[4] survive is through teamwork.

They huddle together in groups, as many as five thousand of them, to keep warm in the frigid and dark Antarctic winter. About eleven can occupy each square yard, and they alternate their positions so no bird is continually on the outside.[5]

Cooperation also comes naturally for swans. When swans migrate, they fly in a V-formation, which reduces wind resistance on the birds that fly farther back in the formation. Because they take turns leading, twenty-five birds can fly 70 percent farther than can one swan alone.[6]

The ptarmigan is a bird that doesn't migrate, but remains in the north year-round. In winter it gets a camouflage of white feathers on its body and extra feathers on its feet that act as snowshoes. In spring, the "shoes" come off and it grows its brown feathers again.[7]

As animals in cold climates have been provided ways to survive the freezing temperatures, those that live in hot climates have also been provided ways to survive. Elephants use their built-in fans, flapping their big ears back and forth to keep cool.[8]

Camels, known as the "ships of the desert," rarely get thirsty. "A camel can go without water for days or even months."[9] Even the feet of a camel help it survive in the desert. Each foot has two big toes that spread apart, preventing them from sinking into the sand.[10]

Equally equipped for water shortages is a certain frog that lives in the central Australian desert. It emerges from its underground den on the few occasions it rains. Absorbing up to 50 percent of its body weight in water, the frog resembles a small balloon and is ready to weather the next drought.[11]

The eagle, too, takes advantage of rain storms—but in a different way. Fashioned for the environment, an eagle's wing construction allows it to ride upon wind updrafts. So instead of being in danger during a storm, the eagle can fly even higher than under fair weather conditions.[12]

Unlike the eagle, some animals don't have to activate their survival systems. The coat of a helpless fawn provides it with camouflage. Its more than three hundred white spots against a tan background hide it well, and since the fawn has no odor, predators pass it by.[13]

Protective coloring, in fact, helps many animals to survive. A chameleon that is completely blind will take on the color of its environment[14]—its color is controlled by body chemicals.[15] Most fish have lighter colors on their undersides to blend in with the light when viewed from below. They're darker on top to blend in better with the underwater plants and mud when seen from above. The Nile catfish, however, which swims upside down to keep an eye on the plants growing on the water's surface, is outfitted with a belly that is darker than its back.[16]

Living things are equipped with built-in survival techniques but are incapable of undergoing major changes—even if demanded by their environment. That's why some species become endangered. True, "there's evidence of a mechanism that produces minor variations."[17] If, for example, a certain species of rabbit comes in two colors, the color that offers the best protection in a certain area will become dominant. But there's "no distinct mechanism for the really creative kind of evolution, the kind that builds new body plans and new complex organs."[18] Leopards can't erase their spots and brightly-colored parrots can't turn brown. Animals can only make the adaptations needed to survive if their gene pool contains the genetic variations for a certain trait.

 For this reason, "the clearest and simplest evidence of creation is 'the marvelous fit of living things to their environment.'"[19] God used incredible creativity in designing each living creature so it could survive and thrive in the climate and environment in which it is placed. God is also very good at providing for our survival in unfavorable circumstances. A God who is capable of such marvels and whose character is perfect deserves our praise and adoration.

DOES IT MATTER?

Kristi was shocked, heartbroken, angry, and confused. Her father had taken her out to breakfast. In the middle of eating pancakes, he told her that he'd decided to divorce her mother. He was going to marry his secretary, who was going to have his baby. His assurances that he loved his children and would always be there for them seemed hollow and insincere. He said he'd already informed Kristi's mother and her brothers the night before when Kristi had been out with her friends.

When they got home from the restaurant, Kristi's dad finished packing his stuff and left.

Kristi's mother cried for days; her junior-high brother, Tom, got into trouble at school; her sophomore brother, Nathan, clammed up and kept everything inside. Kristi's prayers were desperate: "God, where are you in all of this? What can I do?"

VITAL INFORMATION

What can we do to cope with the long-term problems over which we have no control? One answer is to turn our attention away from the crushing circumstances and concentrate on the greatness of God. Meditate on the grandeur of the One who carved out the mountains, planted the jungles, and fashioned the beautiful beaches.

Reflect, too, on the compassion, strength, and goodness of God. He has rescued prostitutes, transforming them into women of God. He has freed drug addicts to live for Him, and He has healed the emotional wounds of those who have suffered horrible abuse or injustice.

Although the Creator has given all humans the dignity of free will, there is no limit to what He can do for the person totally committed to Him. Discovering in a profound way who God is and how He revealed Himself in His Son makes all the difference.

> Turn your eyes upon Jesus,
> Look full in His wonderful face,
> And the things of earth will grow strangely dim
> In the light of His glory and grace.[20]

IF KRISTI LEARNS TO PRAISE GOD
WITH SINCERITY, THE NEXT
CHAPTER OF HER LIFE COULD READ
LIKE THIS . . .

And things got worse for Kristi and her family before they got better. Kristi's mother had to sell their house, and they moved into a townhouse. Kristi's mother also became more and more bitter. Tom's rebellion increased, and Nathan was being treated for depression. The day the divorce was final, her father and his secretary went to Las Vegas to get married. Kristi felt like the pressure was more than she could take.

Then she met Megan, whose aunt and uncle attended Kristi's church. Megan had come from California to live with them, and she also attended Kristi's high school. Megan lived her Christianity more than anyone Kristi had ever known. Her kindness and her joy were contagious. She wasn't afraid to tactfully present Christian viewpoints in hostile classrooms, and she had an incredible capacity to care for other people.

Megan saw that Kristi was struggling and went to visit her.

"I thought it might help you," said Megan, "if you heard my story." Four years before, Megan had lost both of her parents and her sisters in a car crash. She'd been living with her grandparents since then, but now their health had failed to the point that they needed to move to an assisted living complex. "What I've discovered," Megan said simply, "is that when I praise God and think of all His wonderful qualities, my problems become smaller and His power increases in my life. I listen to praise music, or I sing hymns or read psalms. I thank God for all the blessings I have, or tell Him how much I appreciate each of His character traits.

"Once I've spent time praising Him, I realize how powerful God really is and that I can ask Him for things with real faith. Of course, some situations are like scrambled eggs; you can't turn them sunny-side up again. For these I let the Lord give me the strength and wisdom to cope. But there are so many things that our prayers can impact."

Kristi listened for all she was worth. Megan was living proof that what she was saying was true. And Kristi was ready to learn to praise God in spite of the situation.

When you need supernatural aid to get through each day, remember that the God who made provision for animals to survive in their environments will provide you with what you need to survive in yours. You can keep on praising Him for what He has done, what He is doing, and what He will do. Praise God because He deserves it—and because you were made to adore Him. You'll find contentment doing what you were designed to do.

Someone has said, "The answer to loneliness isn't love—it's praising God." Try it. Only God can fill the emptiness inside, and praise connects you with Him. Learn to continually worship God with the way you work and study, in your responses to frustrations, by focusing moment to moment your attention on Him. It will transform your life.

ACTION STEPS TO EXPERIENCING THE POWER OF PRAISE

1. Decide to stop mulling over your problems and write down all the qualities that God possesses.
2. Read about the greatness of God in the Psalms, especially in these Psalms: 19; 23; 27; 34; 37; 43; 50; 62; 86; 91; 100; 107; 113; 139; 146.
3. Spend ten minutes thanking God for major things like sending Jesus to die on the cross for you, and for minor things like providing money to buy a snack or helping you with a pop quiz.
4. Before you bring each request to God, praise Him and thank Him for what He is going to do.

WORDS TO LIVE BY

Praise the LORD. Give thanks to the LORD, for he is good; his love endures forever.

—Psalm 106:1

The LORD is good to all;
he has compassion on all he has made.
All you have made will praise you, O LORD;
your saints will extol you.

—Psalm 145:9–10

HE'S PERFECT—
THAT IS GOD

DID YOU KNOW?

Plants and trees have some pretty impressive qualities.

California redwoods, for instance, "are the world's tallest living trees. . . . a redwood in northern California is the tallest known living tree in the world. It is about 368 feet high."[1] Yet the redwoods, which achieve such colossal growth, start from seeds that are only one-sixteenth of an inch long—seeds so small that it takes 123,000 of them to make a pound.[2]

The General Sherman tree in California's Sequoia National Park is the largest tree—in terms of volume—in the world and weighs more than six thousand tons.[3] It is 274.9 feet tall, 102.6 feet in circumference at its base, and has a volume of 52,058 cubic feet.[4]

Another superior sequoia, the General Grant, could supply enough wood to build fifty, six-room houses.[5] The height of this enormous tree is about 268.1 feet, with a circumference at its base of 107.6 feet, and a volume of 46,608 cubic feet.[6]

Trees not only achieve impressive size, but set age records as well. Sequoias live to be a record-setting age of more than two thousand years old, taking 500 to 750 years for them to reach their full height of 250 or more feet. That's equal to at least a twenty-five-story building.[7]

It is now illegal to cut down sequoia trees, but in one that was felled, the central growth ring dated back to 1305 B.C.[8] The famous "Constable Tree," an orange tree brought to France in 1491, lived and bore fruit for 473 years.[9]

Maple trees, too, have some outstanding qualities. A mature maple tree may have as many as 146,250 leaves, and the leaves on a single acre of grown trees will collect enough solar energy to supply fifty homes with electricity for a full year. Maple trees that are tapped for their sap have to work harder, but they end up producing more sugar water than those that are left untapped. After being tapped for 50 to 100 years, tapped trees develop fatter trunks than those left untouched.[10]

Besides giving us food, lumber, and other useful products, trees also have other beneficial qualities. Their roots hold soil in place; through photosynthesis, trees help supply our planet with oxygen; they provide us with shady places on hot days. Trees also expel moisture into the air. In one twenty-four-hour period, a large oak tree gives off ten to twenty-five gallons of water through its leaves.[11]

Bamboo in its seven hundred different varieties[12] is used by more people for more purposes than any other plant on Earth.[13] A typical farmer in Southeast Asia could live in a bamboo house, sit in bamboo chairs, eat food prepared in bamboo containers, sleep on a bamboo mat using a bamboo "blanket," and wear sandals made from bamboo strips. His pigs and chickens might live in bamboo cages while a bamboo fence encloses his yard. Bamboo sprouts are eaten as vegetables. Rafts, sails, fishing poles, rope, paper, and baskets are also made of bamboo. An amazing quality of bamboo is its strength. Layered bamboo is so strong that its breaking point nearly equals that of soft steel.[14]

An estimated 75,000 plant species in the world provide food. The number that have ever been cultivated by humans, though, is calculated to be a mere 7,000.[15] One of those plants is the soybean, which is currently gaining a reputation for its many uses. Most people think of soybeans as something to eat, but they're also used in products as diverse as candles, soap, varnish, cosmetics, and textiles. Still, the soybean has qualities that make it a desirable addition to the diet of both humans and animals. After processing, soybeans contain about forty percent protein (compared with 18 percent for beef and chicken), and soybeans are cheap. Furthermore, soybean oil contains no cholesterol and has the lowest level of saturated fat among the vegetable oils. You may, in fact, eat more soybean products than you realize. Food labels show that soybeans contribute to things like margarine, salad dressings, and even candy and ice cream.[16]

Not many of us, however, are big fans of soybeans—we have other favorites that are more well known for their outstanding flavor. Most would agree that strawberries, peaches, corn on the cob, and peanuts are among God's tastiest creations.

Not only did the Creator make many plants for the purpose of producing outstanding eating, He also created plants of incredible beauty. Consider the grace of a perfectly shaped weeping willow, the serenity induced by a velvety carpet of grass dotted with wildflowers, the intoxicating scent from a row of lilacs laden with blooms. There are a quarter of a million species of flowering plants, including dewy pink roses, soaring sunflowers, deep purple petunias—and 249,997 more![17]

Something innate in every human recognizes outstanding performance, beauty, and quality. Growth records are seldom set by stunted redwood trees, the blue ribbon at a rose show never hangs on a pot of weak blooms, no pie made from shriveled and bitter fruit ever took first prize at a county fair. The person who'd declare that a patch of mud is more beautiful than a well-tended flower garden in full bloom would be considered odd.

Some people would have us believe that there's no such thing as good and bad, that everything is relative and subjective. If that were so, we wouldn't recognize what's outstanding and what's merely ordinary or even inferior. Where, then, did this universal sense of perfection and beauty come from? It originated with a perfect Being who stamped His definition of perfection and beauty on the universe that He made.

DOES IT MATTER?

Marissa and Sara sat in their social studies class. Mr. Jones was summarizing what he'd said during the period.

"The oriental view of life is an example of a perspective on which we can build a new world order to ensure peace. It's the most tolerant, proclaiming that everything—even good and evil—is part of God. Since nothing is bad, there's no need to look down on anyone for his or her behavior or beliefs. Since all human beings are also part of God, no one is left out and every opinion is of equal value."

When he looked at his watch, Mr. Jones concluded his lecture and wrote the assignment on the board: "Write a two-page essay on your idea of a perfect world."

The bell rang, and Marissa and Sara headed for their lockers. "It should be obvious to Mr. Jones, and to everyone else," said Marissa, "that evil really exists. That's why we'll never have a perfect world."

"Judge not that you be not judged," Sara quipped. "And that's from the Bible. Who are you to say that what Mr. Jones or anybody else thinks is incorrect?"

"If something goes against the Bible, it's wrong—no matter who says it," Marissa insisted.

"You've been brainwashed! You sound so narrow-minded. Can't you see that some parts of the Bible don't fit modern society?" Sara preached. "I go to church too, but I still hold on to my brain and my heart."

Since Marissa and Sara were good friends, Sara's words hurt Marissa and left her confused.

VITAL INFORMATION

God is perfect, and He created a perfect world. But he gave Adam and Eve the right to choose how they would live. When they chose to sin, evil entered creation and changed our planet for the worse. But God sent a Savior to die for our sins and to give each person, who so chooses, the opportunity to regain everything Adam and Eve forfeited in the Garden of Eden.

For those who accept Christ, the process of inner transformation begins now, but it will be completed only in heaven. "Salvation comes from the LORD" (Jonah 2:9), so it's impossible for us to save ourselves or to build a perfect world on Earth. Yet God put within each of us the ideals of perfection and the sense that something is terribly wrong with life as we know it. He did this not so we'd come up with philosophies that change the definition of right and wrong, but so that we'd individually come to Him to be forgiven and changed and started on the road to what's right. Then we can spread this good news.

IF MARISSA SEEKS OUT GODLY ADVICE, HER DAY COULD END WELL . . .

Unsure of herself, Marissa decided she should meet with her youth pastor. She used her cell phone to set up an appointment with him for that afternoon, then she let her mom know why she'd be home later than usual.

Pastor Gary listened to Marissa's story. "I'm glad you came to talk," he said. "What you're experiencing is a clash of worldviews. A lot of people don't believe that the whole Bible is true, and they don't know about the power of Jesus to transform lives. They assume it's *their* job to create a utopia or paradise on earth. Communism was such a system. It assumed that equally redistributing all the wealth would create peace and eliminate severe poverty."

"That's kind of like some Muslims today," Marissa said, "the one's who want to build their own version of a perfect world. My dad said that the radical ones feel justified in 'holy war,' because people who resist Islamic rule are considered infidels, who are obstacles to peace. They believe that peace will come about when there is total submission to Allah."

"Yes, each group has their own idea about how to impose world order," Pastor Gary said. "Present views on a one-government world go back at least to Alexander the Great, a student of Aristotle. His idea was to unify the people of his empire by making everybody learn the Greek language, adopt Greek culture, and embrace a common religion. To his credit, he sought to promote his ideas through persuasion rather than violence.

"The Romans had a similar philosophy. Part of it was a 'you-accept-our-religion-and-we'll-accept-yours' compromise. Since the Romans were pagans and worshiped many gods, and the majority of people they conquered were pagans who worshiped a bunch of gods, no one thought that adding a few more gods was a big deal. Jews and Christians, though, worshiped only one God, and they got into trouble."

"But what can I write in my essay?" said Marissa. "If I say that I believe in the Bible, Mr. Jones will probably think I'm crazy."

"If it were me," Pastor Gary advised, "I'd start with a paragraph defining a perfect world. The Bible's description of heaven will give you great ideas. Explain the systems that people in the past have used to try to create paradise on Earth and tell why each failed."

"Okay. That sounds good," Marissa said as she scribbled some notes. "Then what?"

"Mr. Jones seems taken with Eastern philosophies," said Pastor Gary. "Do you think those philosophies have resulted in a perfect society?"

"Of course not," said Marissa. "India has the caste system, and their idea of karma results in lack of concern for the poor. Many Eastern countries don't respect women or give women many rights, and I've read about the actions of militant Hindus." Marissa wrote more notes and said, "Come to think of it, I don't see how Mr. Jones thinks that Eastern thought is a good foundation for peace on Earth."

"You might end your essay," said Pastor Gary, "with your thoughts on how people can even approach a perfect existence."

"I think the perfect world will never happen here on Earth," said Marissa. "People need to let God totally change them from the inside out, then they'll be able to live in heaven. And heaven is a different dimension, where we won't have death and pain and frustration. Right?"

"That's what Christians believe, Marissa," said Pastor Gary. "But a lot of people don't agree with us."

"Thanks, Pastor Gary," Marissa smiled and closed her notebook. "Now that I realize where Sara—and just about everyone else—is coming from, I won't take their comments personally. I can take a stand for the Bible and for the truth."

All people recognize standards of beauty and goodness, causing them to strive for things like peace and a better world. What is the source of these ideals? The poet Joyce Kilmer—perhaps inspired by a stately oak, or a pine frosted with snow, or an apple orchard in full bloom—exclaimed, "Only God can make a tree!" And a tree is just one of many examples of God's perfection in nature.

If you, like Marissa, realize that only God is capable of perfection and that He gave us our ideals for living in a perfect world, you'll see that an earthly paradise can never be achieved by human effort. You can be active in working to improve your corner of the universe, and through prayer and Spirit-led action you can and should resist evil. But the primary goal is spreading the gospel and attempting to bring your friends and relatives to heaven with you.

ACTION STEPS FOR INFLUENCING A SINFUL WORLD

1. Let the Bible give you your picture of Earth's reality.
   - Genesis 3:1–19
   - Isaiah 43:11–13
   - Jeremiah 17:9
2. Realize that through God's power you can win victories—no matter what!
   - Luke 10:19
   - Romans 8:37
   - 2 Corinthians 2:14–16
3. Decide to use your influence positively.
   - Matthew 5:13–16
   - Galatians 6:10
4. Ask God to guide you in resisting evil and doing good.
   - Luke 6:31, 36
   - Ephesians 4:32

WORDS TO LIVE BY

> I will proclaim the name of the LORD.
>   Oh, praise the greatness of our God!
> He is the Rock, his works are perfect,
>   and all his ways are just.
> A faithful God who does no wrong,
>   upright and just is he.
>
> —Deuteronomy 32:3–4

Do not be overcome by evil, but overcome evil with good.

—Romans 12:21

The prayer of a righteous man [or woman] is powerful and effective.

—James 5:16

THE WORLD YOU CREATE WILL FALL APART

DID YOU KNOW?

Mutations are small changes in living things. Mutations are rare—perhaps one in every 10 million duplications of a DNA molecule (10^7).[1] Observable—that is, major—mutations cause certain kinds of cancer and brain malfunction as well as genetic defects such as hemophilia, which prevents the blood from clotting normally.

Every significant change in the structure of a plant or animal would require a *series* of favorable, related mutations. The odds of four related mutations occurring (which wouldn't make a dent in changing a frog into a crocodile) would be one in 10^{28}.[2] And if life evolved from a single cell, it would have taken trillions of mutations to produce present life forms. Since there are only 10^{80} atoms in the whole universe, the Earth isn't big enough to hold the number of organisms necessary for making the odds of this happening likely.[3]

Moreover, if a living creature were to change its structure through a series of tiny mutations, it would take an enormous amount of time. Five billion years (the time period some assign to the evolutionary process) sounds like a long time, but it's only 10^{17} seconds.[4] "Even by the wildest 'guesstimates' the universe isn't old enough or big enough to reach odds like 1 in $10^{3,000,000}$ that Huxley, an evolutionist, estimated as the odds against the evolution of a horse."[5]

Mutations require not only vast time and numbers of organisms, they also require a change in DNA programming. Although there is allowance for variety within each species, as seen in the many different breeds of dogs, "no existing DNA programming for a species *change* [emphasis added] exists"[6]—if your definition of *new species* requires the creation of genetic information.

Microbiologists know about these probability statistics and DNA programming. For this reason, they have given up on their research that was based on the idea that mutations were responsible for bacteria becoming resistant to antibiotics. It was discovered that some bacteria were resistant *before* the antibiotics were developed and those bacteria passed this resistance on to their friends.[7]

Even though a very few mutations are favorable to survival, mutations are, nonetheless, defects—a loss or corruption of information.[8] If you were to ask for an example of a documented mutation that *increased* DNA information content, you'd stump the experts, at least the honest ones. Mutations are, then, harmful at least one thousand times more often than they are helpful.[9] Finding a mutation that is favorable under all circumstances is, then, quite a challenge. Sometimes sickle-cell anemia, a disease of the red blood cells, is mentioned as a favorable mutation. It does make carriers immune to malaria, but 25 percent of children who have sickle-cell anemia die from it—not at all a positive outcome.[10]

If observable mutation occurred in the distant past, an abundance of missing link fossils should prove that such mutations really happened. "Millions upon millions of fossils have been recovered since Darwin . . . [and] not a single 'missing link' clearly demonstrates the transition from one reproductive species to another."[11] It, in fact, takes more credulity to believe that—through favorable mutations brought about by random chance—a frog evolved into a prince than to believe that God is the designer and creator of everything.

Yet there's something within each human that tends to leave God out of the equation—whether we want to explain the origin of the universe, find the right person to marry, or solve the problems of daily life. Some Christians would look at drawings that try to demonstrate how an ameba evolved into a man, and they'd think that the people who believe in this kind of evolution are terribly gullible. Yet these same Christians can become functional atheists when it comes to trusting God to run their lives.

DOES IT MATTER?

Danae was pleased when Kelly showed up at church. Kelly was a new girl at school, and she was in three of Danae's classes. Danae had been longing for a close Christian friend at school. It was lonely being the only one determined to live out Christianity even if others mocked or socially isolated her. She invited Kelly to spend the weekend with her family at their lake cabin.

"Did your mom say you could go?" Danae asked the next day.

"No," replied Kelly.

"That's too bad," Danae said, "but there'll be other opportunities to go with us."

"Oh, I'm going, all right," Kelly said. "I just need to talk my mother into it." Seeing the surprised look on Danae's face, she continued, "Don't look so shocked. Stop by my house on your way home so I can give you a definite answer, and we can make our plans then."

Unsure of herself, Danae accepted the invitation. Kelly's mom greeted them from the study where she was working on her computer. Kelly's eyes filled with tears.

"Is something wrong dear?" her mother asked.

That released a flood of tears. "You divorced my dad and took him away from me," Kelly sobbed. "And now you want to deprive me of all the little joys of life, too. Dad was never this strict. I wish I lived with him."

"Okay, Kelly," her mom sighed, "if it means that much to you, I'll let you go with Danae's family."

As she walked Danae to the door, Kelly grinned and commented, "It works every time."

VITAL INFORMATION

"If you always do what you like, pretty soon you won't like what you do."

Becoming a slave to your desires is the worst kind of bondage. A spoiled child is an unhappy kid, a self-centered person has few friends, and a stubborn individual suffers for refusing to take advice. The "world of me" becomes a prison, and you need to know how to escape.

IF KELLY LISTENS TO GODLY ADVICE, THESE CHANGES COULD OCCUR . . .

Kelly was a fun-loving girl, and Danae's family enjoyed having her at the cabin. She even took the time to teach Danae's little brother a couple new songs on the guitar. Danae found that they could talk about spiritual things and that Kelly knew her Bible well. When Danae asked her dad for permission to take the rowboat out on the lake, he made them promise not to take off their life jackets and to be back by 4:30.

The autumn day was perfect. Danae and Kelly felt as if they were rowing across a mirror. The blazing colors of the trees in the surrounding hills were reflected upon the surface of the water. Kelly wanted to explore the public park on the opposite shore.

"We can't," Danae protested. "We have to be back by 4:30."

"But we can always invent a damsels in distress story," Kelly countered. "I don't want to go back just yet."

"Kelly, have you really accepted Christ as your Savior?" Danae asked.

Surprised, Kelly shot back, "Why do you ask?"

"How can you be so deceitful?" Danae wondered out loud, trying not to sound harsh.

"If I just meekly obeyed all the time," Kelly countered, "I'd never get to do what I want."

"It's not just the hypocrisy and the lying that bothers me." Danae decided to level with her. "It's like you're trying to manipulate everybody . . . to control them. The Bible teaches that we're supposed to honor our parents and respect authority. Rebellion is extremely dangerous."

"Well, I don't like to be bossed around," Kelly said. "I've been throwing tantrums since I was two, so I guess it's just normal for me to rebel."

"When I started middle school," recalled Danae, "I developed the habit of complaining about almost everything. One day my mother took me to visit Mrs. Campbell. She never stopped complaining the whole time we were there. She fretted about the hot weather and she fumed about the high cost of prescription drugs. Then she complained about the younger generation, and griped about the way her relatives treated her. She even fussed about all the noise her neighbor's dog made. I hated every minute.

"After we left, my mother asked me if I wanted to be like Mrs. Campbell when I grew up. I got the message. I decided to make Philippians 2:14 the motto of my life: 'Do everything without complaining or arguing.' I still repeat it when I start to bellyache about something."

"Well," said Kelly, her voice less adamant, "It's not easy to take orders when you think they're not fair."

Danae looked Kelly straight in the eye. "I'd like you to look into the future. Do you think your future boss or your future husband will enjoy putting up with your dishonesty and your tears and your manipulation? Would you like to have a daughter who gets her way by using tactics like yours?"

"I've never even thought of it that way," Kelly admitted. "I guess it can get kind of ugly."

Danae smiled. "I'm not a perfect daughter either, but if you're serious about changing, I know a verse you could repeat each time you're tempted to get your own way. It's Ephesians 4:25: 'Therefore each of you must put off falsehood and speak truthfully to his neighbor, for we are all members of one body.'"

When they got back to the cabin, Kelly wrote the verse down and they prayed together. Kelly promised God she'd stop exaggerating, fudging on the truth, and turning on the crocodile tears. Danae prayed for her and said she'd continue to do so.

But Kelly found it hard to change. It was like she was addicted to manipulation. Even with prayer and memorized Bible verses, she fell back into the old pattern. She decided she could best break her bad habits by obeying her mother without question—unless she felt that there was a good reason to present her side in a calm, rational, and respectful way.

Sometimes she was able to stop herself before she began a tirade. She realized what was happening and forced herself to apologize to her mom. Once she even abruptly stopped her crying and told her mother she would obey. But change was a long hard struggle.

Just before Christmas, Kelly informed Danae, "I can't go to the youth league bowling party because my mom can't give me the money—but I'm letting God take care of me. I'll see you Sunday in church."

"I'm so proud of you," Danae said as she hugged her. "Obeying God's Word is changing you into a different person. I'm sure that when you meet Mr. Right, you'll be glad that you decided to conquer manipulation."

Have you, like Kelly, developed habits that are hard to change, habits that defy principles set down by the Designer of the universe? Do you act as if you know more than God Himself? Change in our personal lives can be as hard to produce as change in the natural world.

But consider—is it rational for you to decide that you can run your life better than the God who loves you unconditionally? This is the God who knows everything there is to know, and who has the whole world in His hand.

In the natural world, the creatures that God designed have very limited ability to make choices for change. But He gave you the freedom to decide—and to plug into His power in order to live differently. Change isn't always easy, but with God, nothing is impossible.

ACTION STEPS TOWARD CONQUERING THE "I'LL-DO-IT-MY-WAY" SYNDROME

1. Realize that the God who designed you and loves you no matter what made all His rules for your good. Because He is all-powerful, He can take care of any fallout from obeying God-ordained authority figures—parents, teachers, church leaders,

and government officials—whenever they ask you to do something that doesn't violate a command of God.

2. Think of the worst spoiled brat you know. Whenever you're tempted to manipulate or to throw a tantrum to get your own way, think of yourself as a grown-up version of that child. Then pray that God will help you conquer manipulation.

3. List the requests and rules of parents, teachers, and church leaders that you inwardly resist or outwardly rebel against. After each one, write Colossians 3:17: "And whatever you do, whether in word or deed, do it all in the name of the Lord Jesus, giving thanks to God the Father through him." Then write down what you would do in each situation if you obeyed this verse of Scripture.

WORDS TO LIVE BY

Do not offer the parts of your body to sin, as instruments of wickedness, but rather offer yourselves to God, as those who have been brought from death to life; and offer the parts of your body to him as instruments of righteousness.

—Romans 6:13

Who is going to harm you if you are eager to do good? But even if you should suffer for what is right, you are blessed. Do not fear what they fear; do not be frightened.

—1 Peter 3:13–14

THE BIG IMPACT
OF LITTLE THINGS

There's no such thing as a "simple cell." A single living cell is "an entire modern factory squeezed into a space one-thousandth the size of the period at the end of this sentence."[1]

Nor is the composition of a cell at all simple. All cells are made up of molecules, which are comprised of atoms, which contain not only protons, neutrons, and electrons but over two hundred subatomic particles that are even smaller. About twenty common elements—especially carbon, oxygen, hydrogen, nitrogen, phosphorus, and sulfur—account for 99 percent of the dry weight for each living cell.[2]

Yet the stuff of which a cell is composed doesn't explain the mystery of life. "Organisms are so complex that no biologist can claim to understand them completely."[3] What goes on within a living cell, in fact, boggles the mind. The cells of the human body—and most other organisms—have their own internal biological clock. These clocks switch on and off in never-varying cycles every twenty-two to twenty-six hours, and they tell the organism when to wake, when to sleep, and maybe even when to die. The clocks function like hourglasses, in that it takes a certain amount of time for clock proteins to pass through. When these clock proteins bunch together and enter the cell nucleus, the process is blocked. But once they are eliminated from the nucleus, it's as if the hourglass were tipped over—the process starts all over again.[4]

A cell's protective membrane is thinner than a spider's web and must function precisely, or the cell will die. Also, each cell generates its own electric field, which at times can be larger than that near a high-voltage power line.[5]

The amount of data within each cell of your body would, if it could be published in book form, fill volumes:

> Trillions of those cells, many of them different from each other, [are] organized with intricate architecture and precision engineering into a working machine. . . . Each nucleus . . . contains a digitally coded database larger in information content than all 30 volumes of the *Encyclopedia Britannica* put together. And this figure is for *each* cell, not all the cells of the body put together.[6]

Each cell contains specialized energy factories with miniature "motors,"[7] and these "motors" are the power producers of the cell. They use food as fuel to do their work of producing high energy molecules of adenosine triphospate (ATP), which are used by your cells whenever you decide to think, or run, or eat popcorn.[8] Every cell has hundreds of these tiny motors, each 200,000 times smaller than a pinhead.[9] And because cells don't stockpile fuel, they must make it from food as needed.

But this fuel would do no good without oxygen, because the energy-releasing fire within our cells requires oxygen. It's the job of the hemoglobin-rich, red blood cells—they resemble little red doughnuts—to carry oxygen to the cells. The red blood cells in your body are so numerous that, if laid side by side, they'd go around the equator four times, and as many as one million oxygen molecules are attracted by the hemoglobin in each cell. When oxygen molecules board a red blood-cell limo, you receive the strength you need to exercise or talk on the phone.[10]

It would be difficult to imagine that even one living cell just happened to appear by pure chance—let alone the trillions of specialized cells in one human body.

In contemplating God's incredible attention to detail—as displayed in the complex, microscopic cells He has created—you can be sure that He wants you to pray about every little thing. The Lord is concerned about how you feel and cares about the difficulties you face. God is interested in helping you in any way you need, whether it's overcoming your shyness, or making better choices about what you eat, or knowing how to study for tests.

DOES IT MATTER?

Nolan had a problem that he was able to hide from most people—especially himself. He was addicted to having everybody like him and to avoiding conflict. Easygoing and full of fun, Nolan had a lot of friends, was popular with the girls, and got along well with older people.

Although he had given his life to Jesus and really believed that God's Word was true, Nolan found it difficult not to go along with the crowd. He knew that when the jokes at his lunch table became X-rated, he should leave, but he always stayed and said nothing. And when his social studies teacher asked if anybody in the class believed that the Bible was true, he kept quiet. After the football games, he tagged along with his friends, and he even drank one beer, just to be sociable.

One day, his mom had a talk with him. "Nolan, I worry about you because you're such a crowd-pleaser. I know it hurts when others get mad at you or reject you for doing what's right, but that's the price you must pay. You need to have enough backbone to stand alone, if necessary, so that you don't compromise biblical principles."

As usual, Nolan listened politely and thanked his mother for her advice, but he didn't take it seriously. It was his senior year, and he didn't want to miss out on anything or offend anyone. Besides, he compromised biblical principles only on little things.

Larry offered to pick Nolan up on Friday night for "senior celebration." Without hesitating, Nolan accepted the invitation. It turned out to be a party in an old warehouse with heavy metal music, drugs, and alcohol. Everybody was getting high.

Instead of immediately taking a bus home, Nolan stuck around. *After all,* he told himself, *I'll have only one little beer.* Soon, some of the kids got really high and the party got louder. A few bullies started some trouble, and the police showed up. Nolan escaped through the back door and made it home before his curfew. But he couldn't go to sleep.

In the darkness of his room, he became aware that his go-with-the-flow lifestyle was, in fact, dangerous. He'd always figured that God was for the big stuff, for emergencies. Nolan thought that he could take care of the little decisions by himself. Now he realized how wrong he was.

VITAL INFORMATION

It's a mistake to assume that, because God is so great and powerful, He is unconcerned about your last assignment or the zits you see in the mirror. He not only oversees the intricate and complicated workings of each microscopic cell, He also wants to be involved in the minute details of your life.

The Bible contains these marvelous descriptions of God:

- "[He] daily bears our burdens" (Ps. 68:19).
- "He guides me in paths of righteousness" (Ps. 23:3).
- "Before a word is on my tongue you know it completely, O LORD" (Ps.139:4).
- "He gives strength to the weary and increases the power of the weak" (Isa. 40:29).
- "He is a shield for all who take refuge in him" (Ps. 18:30).

God is willing to listen to all of your problems and will guide you in solving them. He wants to be involved in your decisions—even the little ones. God desires to be the center of your thoughts so that what you say can always glorify Him. He listens to your prayers both for physical stamina to do your best in sports and for moral strength to do what's right—even when no one else is.

When kids make fun of you or someone spreads lies about you, the Lord is on your side. God is the God of every day—the Lord of each detail of life.

IF NOLAN LISTENS TO GOD, THIS COULD BE THE NEXT INSTALLMENT OF HIS STORY . . .

Sunday's sermon hit home. "The sin of fearing what other people will think can get us into tons of trouble," the pastor was saying. "Wanting to fit in with the group in which you find yourself can lead to serious consequences.

"Solomon wanted to be like the other kings, so he married a wife with each political alliance he made. Peter didn't want to stand out as different, so he denied Jesus three times. Pilate wanted to be popular, so he ordered that Jesus be crucified. If you're a crowd-pleaser, remember that you're in some pretty terrible company. But if you confess and sincerely repent, God will forgive you and help you go against the crowd."

Nolan bowed his head and prayed, "Lord, I'm sorry. Please forgive me. Give me Your power to stand up for You." And he meant it. He realized it might cost his popularity—and he was willing to pay the price. He also decided to make a real effort to read the Bible and pray every day.

As he prayed, he realized that he'd never asked God to help him pick his friends, so that became a daily petition. A week later, he heard a guy in the lunch line saying, "When I have a problem, man, I request help from the Creator of the universe and read the Bible to get some answers."

Nolan introduced himself to Mike and asked if he could eat lunch with him. Nolan discovered that Mike was a turned-on Christian from whom he could learn a lot. Of course the other guys got on his case, but this time he told the truth. "That drug party was too much for me. I've never told you guys that I'm a Christian. I know I've been a terrible example, but I hope to change." He knew they would ostracize him—and they did.

In social studies class Nolan had another opportunity to speak out for what he knew was right. In a discussion there, Nolan declared that all human life was valuable because God had created it. Kids looked at him like he was from Mars and started calling him "Preach."

But Nolan had decided that God's opinion of him was the most important. He and Mike started praying together and found three more Christian students with whom to eat lunch. And when Larry and Nolan's other old friends got busted for shoplifting, Nolan thanked God that he'd escaped just in time from the peer pressure-cooker.

The God who watches over each process in each living cell in the universe has the ability and the desire to help you with daily dilemmas, to guide you in each moral decision, and to comfort you when things go wrong. Never decide that God is too busy running the universe to have time to help you study for the big test, to calm you for the job interview, or to give you love for the kid you simply can't stand.

ACTION STEPS FOR RECEIVING GOD'S GUIDANCE IN MAKING DAILY DECISIONS

1. Decide that God's opinion of you matters more than that of anyone else.
2. Read your Bible every day so you know what God thinks about the issues of life.
3. Pray a lot, asking God to choose your friends and to show you who can give you godly counsel for making important decisions.
4. Remember that "little" decisions form habits and patterns for life. Ask God for His wisdom in each one of them.

WORDS TO LIVE BY

> Commit your way to the LORD;
>   trust in him.
>
> —Psalm 37:5

> Trust in the LORD with all your heart
>   and lean not on your own understanding;
> in all your ways acknowledge him,
>   and he will make your paths straight.
>
> —Proverbs 3:5–6

29

LIVING ABOVE
IT ALL

In order to fly, a bird must have more than wings. First of all, birds need feathers, of course. A whistling swan can have as many as 25,216 feathers.[1] And feathers are complicated structures. A flight feather attached to a wing bone can have more than one million parts.[2]

Yet as light as feathers are, those of a bald eagle weigh twice as much as its skeleton. That's because an eagle's bones are hollow and filled with air. The bald eagle is three feet long from head to tail and has a wingspan of seven feet, but it weighs only nine pounds.[3] Its light weight gives an eagle easy maneuverability and allows it ride on wind power to conserve energy. The bird's lightweight bones are also extra thin, its beak is lightweight, and many of its feathers have hollow shafts.

Not only does the bird's anatomy make it built to fly, so does its metabolism. Birds eat energy-rich foods like seeds, fruits, fish, small rodents, worms, and insects.[4] The average robin requires about seventy worms a day.[5] An extra-efficient digestive system allows food to pass through a bird in less than an hour, giving it quick energy. Birds can swallow a lot of food and store it in their crops. Food is digested as needed in their gizzards, which are grinding organs, taking the place of teeth, since teeth would add to their weight.

Birds have other body systems and organs that contribute to their airworthiness. It takes a lot of oxygen to fly, and the lungs of birds take in extra oxygen because of a system of air sacs connected to their lungs. Unlike most animals, birds have fresh air in their lungs both when they inhale and exhale.

The heart of a bird is larger and beats faster in proportion to its size than those of other small animals. The heart of a small bird may beat more than five hundred times a minute, whereas that of a frog beats only twenty-two times a minute.[6] A hummingbird's heart weighs a fraction of an ounce but beats eight hundred times a minute.[7]

The bird's eyes, too, equip it for flight. Some birds can see eight times more sharply than humans, allowing them to dart quickly through trees and branches. In most birds, the eyeballs are larger than the entire brain.[8]

But don't knock those birdbrains. They know how to fly long distances without getting lost. The rufous hummingbird, which is less than four inches long, travels from its Alaskan breeding grounds to Mexico each year—a six thousand-mile round trip—and has no problem finding its way.[9]

It seems obvious to the careful observer that every detail of a bird's anatomy is especially designed for flying. The observer will also note that the ability to fly is a lot more complicated than some reptile's sprouting wings (as if that were simple) and going to flight school. In order to fly, a bird needs a light frame, feathers—birds are the only creatures with feathers[10]—a specialized digestive system, made-to-order heart and eyes, as well as a brain that's wired for flight.

Scientists have found fossil remains of an extinct bird that they named archaeopteryx. Because of a few of its characteristics, the archaeopteryx is cited as proof that birds evolved from reptiles: it has claws on its wings, as do ostriches, plus it resembles the penguin because of its unfused backbone and bony tail. But that doesn't prove that reptiles turned into birds.

Moreover, archaeopteryx had no intermediate characteristics but only fully functional ones. It had completely developed, fully functional wings, for instance, and fully developed and functional feathers. The archaeopteryx had teeth, but since many reptiles don't have teeth and some fossil birds do, archaeopteryx's dentures don't automatically point toward a bird evolving from a reptile.[11] It's more plausible to believe that this bird, like other extinct species, looked a little different from the living forms still around today.

God knew ahead of time the kind of environment that different birds would face and the feats that would be required of them. So He gave them exactly what they'd need to fly and to fulfill their purpose.

God also has a plan for each of us that includes both the temporal and the eternal. He gave us the talents, personality, interests, and spiritual gifts that enable us to fulfill His purpose for us on Earth. And He also gave us a desire to connect with the supernatural, to be immortal, and to accomplish things that will last forever. We want to soar, as on wings of eagles, transcending the ordinary; conquering pain, confusion, weakness, and sadness that, like gravity, pulls us down.

DOES IT MATTER?

A. J. came from an inner-city family. His father had abandoned them, and his mother worked as a waitress. He and his brothers knew what it was like to go without a lot of things. A. J. had to give his mom half his wages from his part-time job. But they had what was most important—a strong faith in God, a close family, and the loving support of genuine Christians in a caring church.

A. J. was a talented artist. He saved for a long time to buy the canvas, brushes, and paints, and he spent three months on the original painting he planned to enter in the citywide contest for a $1,000 prize. His art teacher encouraged him and even stopped by their top-floor apartment to see the finished project and take a few photos. Mr. Carey was impressed. "If you don't win," he said, "I'll be surprised."

"Thanks, Mr. Cary," A. J. said. "I'm lucky to have an art teacher like you. You've helped me a lot."

The weekend before the contest, a missionary conference was held at A.J.'s church. His mother got off work so they could all attend together.

While they watched a movie about missions, a terrible storm came up. The wind howled, the hail beat against the windows, and the rain came down in torrents. A.J.'s mom was worried. She'd asked the landlord several times to fix the roof because of a small leak in the kitchen, and now she wondered if the storm had done some damage.

When the weather calmed down, she asked a man from the church to drive them back to check on the apartment. The kitchen was one big puddle and a gaping hole in the ceiling of the boys' room had let in all the rain. A. J.'s painting was completely ruined.

VITAL INFORMATION

God "has made everything beautiful in its time. He has also set eternity in the hearts of men; yet they cannot fathom what God has done from beginning to end" (Eccl. 3:11).

The observant person will marvel every day at God's creation: a meadowlark trilling an original melody, tulips that cheer the landscape with their bright colors, a snowcapped mountain reflected in a clear lake, a kitten capering in a pool of sunlight. Yet we have a sense that there's something beyond the wonder and beauty of this life. We were made for more than getting up each morning, going through our daily routines, and trying to get eight hours of sleep a night.

God has planned that "you may participate in the divine nature" (2 Peter 1:4). He wants you to receive His love and pass it on to others. He wants you to experience His power of forgiveness and share it as you forgive others. You can gain God's perspective on situations as you let His words in the Bible become real in your life.

Whatever you do at home, or school, or work is an opportunity to reflect Jesus to those around you. And you can help populate heaven in various ways—by giving money in the missionary offering, by sharing your faith with a friend, or by inviting someone to an evangelistic outreach. Instead of being bound by the things of this world, you can be born again, free to fly above that which hinders you from living with eternity's values in view.

IF A. J. GETS GOD'S PERSPECTIVE, THIS COULD BE THE REST OF THE STORY . . .

A. J. was devastated. Taking refuge in the bathroom, he cried for the first time in three years. Then his mind turned to the movie they'd just seen at church. At the end, it showed people wearing beautiful clothes, living in impressive homes, driving new cars, enjoying luxurious vacations and top-brand sporting equipment. The narrator asked, "And of what value will these things be to you in a hundred years?"

Earlier in the film were scenes of missionaries teaching the Bible to primitive tribesmen, a girl leading her friend in a prayer to accept Christ, a team giving food to starving people, and a lady comforting a grieving neighbor. Next, two verses appeared on the screen: "Whoever turns a sinner from the error of his way will save him from [eternal] death" (James 5:20) and "Whatever you did for one of the least of these brothers of mine, you did for me" (Matt. 25:40).

Reflecting on the truth that the movie portrayed, A. J. told God that he planned to live the rest of his life focused on the things that would last forever—and God certainly honored his commitment. Friends at church found out about what had happened. They raised a thousand dollars and presented it to A. J. Mr. Carey enlarged a photograph of A.J.'s painting and gave it to him. The insurance money not only enabled the landlord to put on a new roof but it also paid for the things damaged by the storm.

But best of all, Mr. Carey was so impressed by A. J.'s attitude that he inquired about his faith. He and A. J. talked about God and about the Bible, and about how to know Jesus personally. A. J. invited Mr. Carey to church and, there, Mr. Carey made a commitment to Christ.

God had used the destruction of something temporal to allow A. J. to have a part in bringing someone to Jesus. The person who dies with the most stuff doesn't win. The real winner is the one who's bound for heaven and whose substantial investments of time, energy, and money are already there.

Whenever you see a bird in flight, pray that God will help you live a gravity-defying life—one that will concentrate on the eternal rather than the temporal. The one who created the birds to fly over the mud, dirt, and slush of earth will supply you with the spiritual resources to rise above difficult problems and depressing circumstances.

ACTION STEPS FOR ACCUMULATING HEAVENLY TREASURE

1. Refuse to allow material things to play a central role in your life.
2. Determine your priorities by placing little importance on the things that won't matter a hundred years from now.
3. Invest your time, talent, and treasure in things that will last forever.
4. Make soul-winning the goal of your life—pray for unsaved friends, tell them what Christ has done for you, invite them to evangelistic events, take a course in personal evangelism, etc.

WORDS TO LIVE BY

Do not store up for yourselves treasures on earth, where moth and rust destroy, and where thieves break in and steal. But store up for yourselves treasures in heaven. … For where your treasure is, there your heart will be also.

—Matthew 6:19–21

Therefore we do not lose heart. Though outwardly we are wasting away, yet inwardly we are being renewed day by day.

—2 Corinthians 4:16

30

FINDING SOME ANSWERS

There are tens of trillions of cells in your body.[1] Each living cell is a collection of several billion molecules made up of a few simple elements.

When the body can't get the necessary food and oxygen, or when the body's operational or repair mechanisms fail, inherent chemical processes cause death—even though all the molecules needed for life are still present.[2] Molecules are, in reality, nonliving.

Our bodies might be compared to a Boeing 747. The 747 has 4.5 million nonflying parts, owing its ability to fly to advanced engineering. In a similar way, our lives depend not upon what we are made of but upon design and organization.[3] "It's not the stuff ['dust'] we're made of that makes us special; it's the way we're put together."[4] We didn't just happen; we were designed.

In order for life to occur, three kinds of molecules need to work in harmony. The "molecules responsible for life chemistry cannot function by themselves. DNA (molecules that hold the blueprints for the construction of life molecules), proteins (molecules that follow portions of the blueprints in building and repairing life molecules), and RNA (molecules that carry the blueprints from the DNA to specific proteins) are all interdependent."[5] If there's no intelligence behind the universe, these three kinds of complex molecules that are necessary for life would need to appear spontaneously and simultaneously from inorganic stuff.[6]

You began as a single cell. Although that cell was smaller than the period at the end of this sentence, that single cell contained the twenty-three sets of chromosomes you inherited from your parents. Those chromosomes were mysteriously locked up in two tightly coiled strands of DNA. Among other things these strands of DNA include

- 100,000 genes that determine everything about you from eye color to foot size, from blood type to musical aptitude;
- the directions for division and differentiation of cells to make over two hundred different kinds of tissue and organ cells—from toenails to hair.

All of this information is stored in something so tiny that the combined initial single cell DNA of all six billion people on earth today would weigh one-thousandth of an ounce. Yet, the DNA from one cell could be stretched to over five feet in length!

Not surprisingly, this same DNA is super thin—only fifty-trillionths of an inch thick. If all of the DNA from all of the trillions of cells in your body were squeezed together, it could fit inside an ice cube.[7]

The genes within DNA manufacture proteins that do everything necessary to keep you alive.[8] "A typical cell contains thousands and thousands of different types of proteins to perform the many tasks necessary for life, much like a carpenter's workshop might contain many different tools for various carpentry tasks."[9] Each gene knows how to make one kind of protein, so 100,000 genes make 100,000 different proteins.[10]

Clearly, the genius of DNA doesn't consist in its three fundamental ingredients—a sugar, a phosphate, and four different kinds of bases.[11] DNA isn't alive; it's a dead molecule.[12] "The information written in DNA is not a product of DNA. Where did the information come from? Who or what is the author?"[13]

To answer that question, we must take into account the great power, the imagination, the incredible intelligence, and the unbelievable skill it takes to execute ideas that are demonstrated by the Inventor of the special DNA code for each living thing: bacteria, bee, bear, or boy.[14]

(And the DNA of a bee won't program a bear. Nor will the DNA of a shark come up with a skunk—thank goodness.)

"If the DNA sequence of the human genome [yours, for example] was compiled into 1,000-page books (the size of a Manhattan telephone directory), the equivalent of 200 volumes would be needed to hold it all."[15] The vast amount of information contained in the DNA of each person clearly indicates that living things have both a design and a Designer.

It shouldn't be difficult, then, to believe that everything that happens to us fits into the loving plan of God in order to bring about an ultimate good. You can trust the one who promised, "I make known the end from the beginning, from ancient times, what is still to come" (Isa. 46:10).

DOES IT MATTER?

Diana leaned her head into her hands and sobbed. For days she'd operated in a fog—too numb to really get in touch with her feelings. Exactly two weeks before, her father had been severely injured in a car accident. For five long days and nights, he lay unconscious, his life in the balance. She and her friends had prayed fervently for his recovery, but on Saturday morning, he died.

Diana had cried and wondered why. But, surrounded by so many friends and relatives, and with so many things that needed to be done, she hadn't yet felt the full impact of losing her father. Going back to school had been hard. Everyone else seemed to be having so much fun while she wondered if she'd ever be happy again.

But today, when she came home, was the first time she'd found the house empty. Loneliness and longing for her father overwhelmed her. As she cried, she felt her heart would break. How could God allow her father to die? How could such pain and emotional agony fit into His plan?

VITAL INFORMATION

How can Diana's questions—and yours—be answered? If human beings are accidents on the way to extinction, a lot of things will never make sense. But the God who designed a DNA identity to determine the future of each pre-born child also programs and permits the events that will best prepare you for eternity.

God has a greater purpose for each life. That purpose goes way beyond the here and now. We were made for another world—one in which all the questions of existence will be answered. Anything that will bring us closer to God and better prepare us for heaven is God's best—even if it is heartbreaking and impossible to understand.

IF DIANA COOPERATES WITH GOD IN COPING WITH LOSS, HER STORY MIGHT CONTINUE LIKE THIS . . .

The death of her dad made a tremendous impression on Diana. Her father had been the picture of health and vitality. Three weeks before the accident, he'd finished fourth in the local marathon race.

Yet one impact caused by excessive speed left him completely helpless and barely breathing. Diana realized that her eternity might begin at any time. Although she didn't feel like it, she decided to take the advice that her father had given her a month before he died.

"Di," he had counseled seriously after listening to her complaints, "why don't you get to know God better by reading through the New Testament?"

Now Diana set aside time each morning to read a chapter from the Bible and to pray. A lot of questions remained, but little by little she found some answers. Since her mom was having such a hard time, Diana felt she had to be strong and always put on a good front for her little brothers. She was beginning to feel the strain.

But then she read John 11. When Jesus came to the grave of His good friend Lazarus, He had plans to raise him from the dead. Yet, missing His friend and seeing the pain around Him, Jesus wept. That meant it was okay for her to cry—and she sensed Jesus sharing her pain, putting His strong arms around her, and weeping with her. She could let down her guard, knowing that God cared about her tears.

Reading the first chapter of 2 Corinthians, she discovered one purpose for grief: "The Father of compassion and the God of all comfort, ... comforts us in all our troubles, so that we can comfort those in any trouble with the comfort we ourselves have received from God" (2 Cor. 1:3–4).

And in a couple of weeks, Diana was able to put that into practice. Noticing a new girl, alone and silent, at a Saturday evening youth group, Diana sat beside her and started a conversation. "You must be new," she said. "I'm Diana."

"I'm Mallory," the girl mumbled, not looking at Diana.

"I've missed the last few meetings," said Diana. "My father died recently, and my mother began working. So Saturday night is the only time I have to help her clean—"

"Maybe you can tell me why God let my mother die," Mallory blurted out. She glanced around, startled at her own outburst. "My dad and I had to move here to live close to my grandparents," she said quietly and looked back at the floor.

"I'm still having a hard time with those kinds of questions myself," Diana responded. "But I'm reading my Bible, and some things are beginning to clear up." Diana's concern and understanding enabled her to become the friend that Mallory needed to help her through the crisis.

But Diana's situation still wasn't easy. Besides missing her father so much, Diana had to adjust to a new economic reality. She gave her mother a portion of her earnings from her part-time job and hardly had any money for herself. She learned to find stylish secondhand clothes and to pray for specific things she needed. When a lady from her church paid her expenses for the youth retreat in answer to prayer, she started to more fully understand God's ability to provide.

One day her pastor approached her. "Diana," he said, "I can't believe the change in you. You've grown so much closer to the Lord, and you've become so mature. I know your father would be proud of you."

Diana realized that although she'd have to wait until heaven to receive all the answers to her questions, some of them were appearing right before her eyes.

Like Diana, you too can rest secure. God—who invented DNA as a blueprint for reproducing each living thing according to the divine pattern—also has a plan for bringing some good out of each setback you face.

Remember that heaven, according to the Bible, is for those who overcome—but, by definition, an overcomer must have something to overcome. So God will give you enough failure to make you persistent, enough heartache to make you compassionate, enough frustration to help you develop patience, and enough problems to make you into a person of prayer. And He will lead you to a victory over each crisis if you reach out for His assistance, if you're willing to look for His guidance, and if you will follow His advice.

ACTION STEPS TO SURVIVING TRAGEDY

1. Adopt an eternal perspective.
2. Receive God's love and His comfort, instead of pretending to be strong and acting like you have it all together.
3. Look for ways to let God use your tough, life experiences to help others.
4. Ask God to help you make the adjustments that your life requires.
5. Pray for the things you need—emotionally, relationally, spiritually, and physically.
6. Remember that the answer to all your "why" questions will be revealed in heaven.

WORDS TO LIVE BY

Praise be to the God and Father of our Lord Jesus Christ! In his great mercy he has given us new birth into a living hope through the resurrection of Jesus Christ from the dead, and into an inheritance that can never perish, spoil or fade—kept in heaven for you. . . . In this you greatly rejoice, though now for a little while you may have had to suffer grief in all kinds of trials. These have come so that your faith—of greater worth than gold, which perishes even though refined by fire—may be proved genuine and may result in praise, glory and honor when Jesus Christ is revealed.

—1 Peter 1:3–4, 6–7

GOD: UP CLOSE AND PERSONAL

DID YOU KNOW?

You'll never find the end of the rainbow—because a rainbow is actually a circle. We see a rainbow as an arc—a segment of the circle—because the horizon cuts off the rest of the circle from our view. If rain showers have been spotty, not covering the observer's full range of vision, the arc is incomplete.[1]

The rainbow takes the shape of a circle because sunlight has to be bent to make colors. Sunlight is really a mixture of the colors of the rainbow—red, orange, yellow, green, blue, and violet. Usually the colors of sunlight travel together in the same direction, but when the light enters a water drop, it acts like a tiny prism. The colors separate as some curve more than others. Violet light bends the most while red light bends the least. Because of this and other reasons, the inside of a rainbow is violet and the outside is red—unless there's a double rainbow. Sometimes a second, fainter rainbow is seen above the main rainbow. The order of the colors is reversed in this second rainbow because the light has been reflected twice, instead of once, inside the raindrops.[2]

Although they are rare, some rainbows are purple. They occur only before dawn when there are high clouds to scatter blue and violet light.[3]

Rainbows, then, are really a display of light. Another event in nature that provides us with free "light shows" is lightning. At any given moment, about two thousand thunderstorms are in progress on the Earth.[4] So our planet experiences about 100 bolts of lightning a second,[5] with some 250,000 bolts striking the U.S. each day.[6] Each lightning bolt is about six inches wide, and most of them occur in tropical regions.[7]

Lightning is not only powerful and awesome, it is essential to plant life. Plants need nitrogen for survival. Although nitrogen comprises about 78 percent of our atmosphere, it won't naturally combine with anything else. Because of this, plants require the nitrogen in the air to be transferred to the soil as nitrates. Lightning causes nitrogen and oxygen to combine into nitric oxide, which is then changed by the atmosphere into nitrates. In this way, hundreds of millions of tons of nitrates are produced by lightning every year.[8] The approximately 10 million lightning bolts that Earth experiences daily give plants the nitrates they need to grow.[9]

Unlike lightning, rainbows are there just to be admired—and to remind us of God's promise never to send us a worldwide flood. And we can see little rainbows everywhere—in water sprinklers, the spray from a garden hose, fountains, the spray thrown up by ocean waves, and even in a few drops of water hanging from a spider's web. "Two people standing side by side admiring 'the rainbow' are actually seeing light refracted and reflected by different sets of raindrops. Each person sees his or her own special rainbow.[10]

God demonstrates His glory, His power, and His knowledge so many different ways. But it's especially gratifying to reflect on the glory of God—a glimpse of which is seen in things like splendorous northern lights, gorgeous sunsets, misty rainbows, moonlight sparkling on the snow, ice glimmering on branches after a sleet storm.

That's why good observers view nature's spectacles and exclaim, "Out here, I feel closer to God." As light and water give each of us our own individual rainbow, the Lord wants to give every individual a touch of His glory—reflected to each of us in a special way.

DOES IT MATTER?

Vann was very conscientious and tried hard to do what was right. Although he did his best, he never felt he measured up to his father's expectations. When he compared his life to biographies or testimonies of super-Christians, he felt like a failure. Because he didn't go to wild parties, stay around for the dirty jokes, or badmouth school authorities, he didn't fit in at school.

Ms. Watson, one of his teachers, liked to set off class debates. Once she realized that Vann held conservative views, she'd pointedly ask him his opinion on certain issues in class and force him to defend his position—sometimes against the entire class. His peers labeled him old-fashioned and intolerant.

Vann was glad, of course, that he was going to heaven, but he often wondered why being a Christian was so hard. Little did he know that the events of one evening would completely change his perspective.

VITAL INFORMATION

God has two kinds of glory: internal and external. His internal glory consists of His natural perfection, His eternal existence, His unchanging pure character, and His love.

That "God is love" (1 John 4:16) could be one argument in favor of the Trinity, because love can't exist unless there is a giving and receiving of love. Jesus speaks of this love relationship with His Father: "My Father loves me" (John 10:17), and "I honor my Father" (John 8:49).

The external glory of God can be observed in the magnitude and splendor of what He has made—things like

- the created universe.
- various ranks of angels.
- human beings complete with creativity, language capacity, personality, and an automatic breathing apparatus.
- the incredible variety of animals and plants.

In addition, His plan for forgiving, saving, and preparing heaven for mere mortals makes us stand in awe.

In spite of the glory of God shown in nature, nothing on Earth brings more glory to God than a life that is totally transformed by God's grace. Consider these examples:

- former slave trader John Newton, who wrote the song, "Amazing Grace";
- ex-gang member Nicky Cruz, who turned into an evangelist;
- Augustine, a one-time womanizer and pagan philosopher, who became a Christian and is known in history as St. Augustine.[11]

Just as the sunlight reflects on water drops, God's glory can be received by us and spread around. The secret of growing as a Christian and becoming more like Jesus is plugging into God's revealed glory—allowing only Jesus to be our true delight and desire and always thirsting for more of Him.

Part of that Christian growth involves letting Christ represent for us all that is truly valuable and becoming for us the definition of beauty, security, power, true knowledge, and incalculable worth.

When we realize that He is all we need, other things fade by comparison. Temptations lose their power, the world becomes less attractive, and what others think doesn't matter. "And we, who with unveiled faces all reflect the Lord's glory, are being transformed into his likeness with ever-increasing glory, which comes from the Lord" (2 Cor. 3:18).

IF VANN REMAINS OPEN TO GOD, THE NEXT SECTION OF HIS BIOGRAPHY COULD GO LIKE THIS . . .

Vann would be too old next year to attend his church's summer Bible camp. So he was glad that he could get time off work to go this summer. Camp was basically the same as other years—the pine-scented unpolluted air, swimming in the lake, goofing off with the other guys in the cabin, sports events, chapel services, praise songs, and worship times.

On Friday night, however, Pastor Greg gave a powerful talk around the campfire. He spoke about the suffering of Christ and the meaning of the Cross in such a moving way, that more than a few campers had tears in their eyes.

Suddenly, Zach, one of the camp rebels, began to sob, crying out, "I'm a sinner, and I'm so far from God." A counselor put an arm around Zach's shoulder and took him away for a private talk. But each person was so engrossed in a personal experience with God that Zach's emotional response seemed not at all out of place.

Soon, in fact, everyone was kneeling. The power of God was so real—the air seemed heavy with divine substance. Vann felt closer to God than he ever had in his life. He almost heard the Lord telling him, "I'm more valuable than anything else. I have all the power, all the joy, all the peace, and all the purpose you'll ever need. But you must constantly plug into what I have to give you. You've been trying to live the Christian life in your own strength, which is something I've never meant for you to do. Just let Me live through you."

Others were confessing sin, apologizing to counselors, or rededicating their lives to Jesus. The meeting lasted a long time, and even when it ended, a sense that heaven had invaded the camp prevailed. Kids went back to their cabins to pray.

The next day Pastor Greg gave his final talk. "You won't always feel the emotions of this day or the sense of the tangible presence of God," he told them. "But if you remember that nothing is as great, or as important, or as fulfilling as God—and if you constantly try to get to know Him better by spending time with Him each day—your lives will never be the same."

And Vann found that to be true. He kept his morning appointments with God, getting the refills he needed to face each day. He sometimes, of course, skipped devotions, difficult situations still arose, and days occurred when everything seemed to go wrong. But that gnawing, spinning-his-wheels feeling of just barely hanging in there was gone. He'd tasted the reality of the glory of God and knew that he wanted more of Him—and that had become the priority of his life.

Just like God shows each one of us a special personal rainbow, He wants to give you the reality of His power and His presence in a way that is particularly designed for you. Your part is to cooperate with Him by presenting yourself to Him. You are the mold into which He wants to pour His glory and His strength. Part of your cooperation with Him also includes reading your Bible and praying each day, and obeying what God says in His Word, as well as attending church, Bible studies, and other Christian meetings. But, most of all, you must cultivate a hunger for God.

ACTION STEPS FOR FOSTERING AN INTIMATE RELATIONSHIP WITH GOD

1. Set a specific time each day to meet with God in a quiet place.
2. Develop a system for your Bible study. Find books to help you, or concentrate on one book of the Bible by reading a chapter each day and then writing a short summary of that chapter in your own words. When you finish the book, try to read the whole thing through in one sitting—a long book will take several reading sessions.
3. Learn to meditate on Scripture, praying that God will show you everything you should see in a passage or verse.
4. Keep on asking God to show you more of Himself.

WORDS TO LIVE BY

Ascribe to the LORD the glory due his name;
    worship the LORD in the splendor of his holiness.
                                            —Psalm 29:2

Great is the LORD and most worthy of praise. . . .
They will speak of the glorious splendor of your majesty,
    and I will meditate on your wonderful works.
                                            —Psalm 145:3, 5

DECIDING HOW TO VIEW YOUR WORLD

In answering the questions, "How did the universe begin?" and "Where did life come from?" it's important to keep the following in mind.

THE WORD "EVOLUTION" HAS MORE THAN ONE MEANING

Microevolution

On the simplest level, the word *evolution* means "change." And observable changes occur within species, such as differences in breeds of dogs, varieties of roses, and types of finches.

"Natural selection" does take place. That is, the members of a species that have certain protective characteristics will survive and reproduce while those with unfavorable traits may die off. If moths or birds or mammals have the DNA programming for different shades of color, for instance, those with coloring most like the environment will become dominant. This natural selection within species is sometimes referred to as microevolution because it cannot effect major change. A cardinal can not, for example, turn brown unless it has inherited genes that will trigger a major color change.

Evolution as taught in secular schools carries microevolution to its illogical conclusion. It assumes that given enough time small changes can extend into mammoth transformations. But just because selective breeding can produce dogs that are smaller, or have floppy ears, or curly hair, *does not* mean that changes can continue indefinitely without limits until at last a new species, such as man, emerges.

An example of similar reasoning—that over time, small changes can continue until they produce big changes—would start with a high school student who could run 100 meters in fourteen seconds. It's possible for that student to train hard and, for three or four months, add a meter a month to the distance he or she can run in fourteen seconds. But after that, improvement will be very slow. And it's totally illogical to assume that the student will be able to add a meter a month to his or her fourteen-second run as long as the student lives, so that at age seventy-five he or she will be able to run 720 meters in fourteen seconds.

Macroevolution

This is an encyclopedia entry for *evolution:* "Current evolutionary theory holds that all species evolved from a single form of life that lived more than 3.5 billion years ago. Over time ... changes have produced more than 10 million species inhabiting the earth today."[1]

There's no place for a God who has a special purpose for each life in this theory. "Modern science educators ... insist that evolution is an unguided and mindless process."[2]

George Gaylord Simpson, a famous evolutionist, says, "Man is the result of a purposeless and natural process that did not have him in mind."[3] Evolution is based on naturalism, the philosophy that nature is all there is.

Phillip E. Johnson explains in more detail: "If nature is all there is, then nature had to have the ability to do its own creating. Darwinian evolution is a theory about how nature might have done this, without assistance from a supernatural Creator. That is why 'evolution in the Darwinian sense is by definition mindless and godless.'"[4] Some scientists prefer to call this idea macroevolution.

Does it make sense to believe that chance, plus time, plus natural processes can produce anything new? Is it logical to hold that in the past, living things always adapted to their environments, but that today they can not, so they become extinct? Where did the matter used by natural processes come from? These are just a few of the questions that a thinking person might ask.

THE THEORY OF MACROEVOLUTION AND A
BELIEF IN INTELLIGENT DESIGN BY AN ALL-
POWERFUL GOD HAVE ELEMENTS IN COMMON

- **No one made a video of how life began,** giving us all the visual details. For this reason, no one knows exactly what happened.
- **The formation of the universe and the beginning of life—one-time events—cannot be scientifically tested by repeatable experiments that will always come out the same way.**

   Scientific laws are established by performing an experiment many times, using the same methods and getting the same results. Boyle's Law, for example, says, "If the temperature of a gas is constant, then its pressure varies inversely with the volume," which means that if the gas is compressed to half its original volume, its pressure doubles. A thousand experiments would produce the same results.

   A scientific law describes how nature works, and a theory is an explanation of why a law or group of laws function as they do. A theory cannot be considered fact unless it can be scientifically tested. There is no experiment that can confirm evolution or creation.

- **We don't know how God created the cosmos, and there is no natural mechanism that can be observed to show how evolution made everything.**

A PERSON MUST ASK, "IS IT CREDIBLE TO
BELIEVE THAT THE UNIVERSE CAME INTO
EXISTENCE BY ITSELF OR IS IT CREDIBLE TO
BELIEVE THAT GOD CREATED EVERYTHING?"

Macroevolutionists must maintain the hope that a natural mechanism will be found for changing beasts into beauty queens, and must trust in whatever is behind that phenomenon. Faith that God created the universe is easier to come by, because the evidence definitely points to intelligent design.

SCIENTISTS ARE HUMANS WHO MAKE MISTAKES
AND SOME HAVE WANTED SO BADLY TO BECOME
FAMOUS THAT THEY HAVE PERPETRATED FRAUDS

- *Darwin mistakenly theorized that characteristics acquired or lost by use and disuse would show up in heredity.* He theorized that giraffes, which supposedly got their long necks from having to stretch to reach leaves on tall trees, passed down that characteristic to their descendents. Even before the discovery of DNA, scientists realized that heredity couldn't be changed by parental habits or by accidents they suffered. Experiments showed that cutting off rats' tails for twenty generations wouldn't change their offspring, nor would athletes who regularly lift weights pass bigger muscles on to their children.[5]
- **Those who have tried to find a missing link between humans and apes have suffered embarrassment more than once.**

  1. "**Nebraska Man** was an error constructed from the tooth of an extinct pig."[6]
  2. **Piltdown Man**, which was the major evolutionary evidence at the 1925 Scopes' trial, was a fraud.[7] Between 1908 and 1912 someone pieced together parts of a human skull and part of an apelike lower jaw. It was hailed as a missing link fossil found in England. Between 1949 and 1959, however, fluorine tests and other modern analysis showed that the bones weren't more than 750 years old and had been deliberately altered to simulate a fossil.[8]
  3. **Neanderthal Man** was not a beetle-browed, bow-legged, knuckle-dragging ape-man, but rather, a sad victim of arthritis and other diseases.[9]

"SCIENCE IS A TRAIN THAT IS ALWAYS
MOVING" AND ITS THEORIES KEEP CHANGING
AS NEW DISCOVERIES ARE MADE

- The "simple cell" has proven to be incredibly complicated.
- *The more we learn about mutations, the less it seems possible that*

they are responsible for "onward and upward" evolution. Mutations are, in fact, "harmful at least 1,000 times more often than helpful."[10] Francisco Ayula defines a mutation as "an error" in DNA.[11] "The building up of mutations with time poses a serious problem for plants and animals as well as for human beings, and time—evolution's 'hero'—only worsens the problem of mutational decay."[12]

If mutational changes were positive, we should be excited about the mutations that would come about if we destroyed the ozone layer. Instead, people today *know* that more mutations won't improve the human race and, for that reason, they're concerned about possible damage to the ozone layer or, for that matter, having too many X-rays.[13] Few, however, think about how illogical it is for evolutionists to believe that past mutations created advanced forms of life.

- It was once believed that the universe was static and stable, allowing for the infinite time necessary for random chance to come up with new life forms. This belief relied heavily on chance. Einstein realized that the universe is constantly expanding, however, and that it is slowly running down, indicating *that time had a beginning—just as the Bible says.*
- *If a new scientific theory or discovery seems to contradict the Bible, just wait.* More information will prove that theory or discovery is incorrect, and the Bible will again be vindicated as has happened so many times before.

THE BIBLE ISN'T A SCIENTIFIC BOOK, BUT WHAT IT SAYS ABOUT SCIENCE IS TRUE

- *Anything that contradicts what the Bible clearly teaches is false.* It's false, for example, to say that an unborn baby isn't human or that life sprang out of nonlife.
- It's important to recognize the factors that influence biblical interpretation and recognize if more than one interpretation can be given to a certain verse.

- *The Bible conveys concepts in the language people speak and the expressions people use.* Then, as now, language reflects what we see—not scientific reality. If, for example, the local weatherman says, "The sun will set tonight at 6:49 P.M.," he isn't bombarded with e-mails telling him that the sun neither rises nor sets, but that the Earth orbits the sun. We all know what he means. I've heard intelligent people say, "To the four corners of the globe," even though the globe is round and doesn't have corners.

  When Joshua 10:13 reports, therefore, that "the sun stood still," and the poetic allegory in Psalm 19:5–6 likens the sun to a champion that "rises at one end of the heavens and makes its circuit to the other," no one should conclude from those phrases, which express ideas in everyday language, that the Bible teaches that the sun circles the Earth.

- *The Bible contains poetry that has no intention of describing scientific fact.* Psalm 98:8: "Let the rivers clap their hands, let the mountains sing together for joy" isn't meant to be taken literally. Nor is Psalm 114:4, where it says, "the mountains skipped like rams."

- *Like English words, Hebrew words can have more than one meaning.* "This is the day we go to the beach" and "the day of the computer has come" are both correct English sentences. It's obvious, though, that the word *day* doesn't mean the same thing in the two sentences. According to *Strong's Concordance,* the Hebrew word *day* can mean "from sunrise to sunset," "from one sunset to the next," "a space of time," and "age."[14] The meaning of the word in each Bible verse must be determined from the context in which it is used.

  And it's always wise to compare Scripture with Scripture, finding out everything the Bible says about a certain topic in order to come to a conclusion about its meaning.

GOD IS CAPABLE OF DOING ANYTHING HE CHOOSES TO DO

"In the beginning God created the heavens and the earth. . . . And God said, 'Let there be light,' and there was light" (Gen. 1:1, 3). The awesome power of God has no limits. And it shouldn't surprise us if we can't figure out how He created the universe. God describes Himself like this: "My thoughts are not your thoughts, neither are your ways my ways" (Isa. 55:8). His ways are higher than ours.

God created us, however, with curiosity. We ask "how" and "why." Christians never need to fear scientific investigation because when all the evidence is in, God's truth will always be vindicated. You needn't worry that some new discovery will discredit Christianity. Being aware of how some scientific calculations are made will help you realize that new information could easily change them. Science often reaches conclusions by working backward from what can be observed, in the same way that we piece together what happened from the clues we find.

Say, for example, a dead body, outfitted in mountain climbing gear, was discovered on top of Mount Everest. Farther down the mountain the remains of several base camps were visible. Most people would just assume that the deceased was part of a climbing expedition.

Someone might discover, however, that a very rich, influential, and eccentric man had a cousin who could pull strings at the Pentagon. On the rich man's behalf, the cousin was asked to bribe an Air Force pilot and arranged for the newest military rescue aircraft to drop off the rich man and his cameraman on the summit. So it was arranged that the craft would hover for ten minutes, and then draw them up into the plane with specially designed equipment.

But hearing about the photo op, the daughter-in-law of the tycoon offered an even bigger sum of money so the pilot and cameraman would simply drop off the rich man and leave him there! After investigation it was found that the base camps had been left by other climbers. This is a farfetched tale, but you get the idea.

When trying to figure out how God made the universe, creation scientists and others have only the clues that we observe around us. But God has limitless options available and could use any method He chose for creating everything. We sometimes ask, "Did our great God, who can do anything—no matter how impossible—create things strictly within the laws of science we can presently discern or did He go outside of them? Did God create the universe in an aged state?"

Adam, for example, came into being without following the known natural laws. He had no natural birth and no childhood. He was created as a mature male, and was an adult even when he was only minutes old. Jesus multiplied loaves and fish without obeying natural laws, without doing any baking or opening a fish hatchery. If He wanted to, God could have instantly set up a totally functioning universe. Or did He create the physical laws of the universe first and then create everything to obey those laws? Others ask, "Are there forces and factors in outer space that we don't yet understand that will change our concept of the universe?" Just as new information often makes scientists who believe in evolution revise their theories, what creation scientists learn may make them change their theories.

EVOLUTIONISTS AND CREATIONISTS DISAGREE AMONG THEMSELVES ON THE DETAILS OF HOW THE UNIVERSE CAME INTO EXISTENCE

- **Traditional evolutionists agree that nothing more than time, chance, and natural processes are responsible for the cosmos and all living things.**
    1. Some evolutionists believe that, somehow, life began on Earth and *that small mutations occurring over time are responsible for the great variety of plants and animals* that exist today as well as for humans.
    2. Realizing that evidence in the fossil record for missing links and transitional forms is lacking, and that probability statistics make traditional evolution impossible, *some evolutionists hold that giant, sudden changes transformed a single cell into every living thing.* Sometimes referred to as the "happy monster" theory or punctuated equilibrium, this idea requires tremendous credulity, because no such instantaneous, huge change has ever been observed.
    3. *Others argue that life came to us from outer space.* Considering the scarcity of planets and the special requirements that are necessary for a planet to support advanced life, believing life on

Earth originated on another planet requires incredible faith. If that life were only an ameba or a protozoan, it still must be explained how such a simple life form could evolve into so many creatures in such a short time, and why these changes aren't documented by many examples in the fossil record. There's another problem. How was that life form—whatever it is—transported from another planet? It's not likely that anyone envisioned a Noah's ark spaceship bringing animals and humans to planet Earth. But in order to solve the problems of how advanced or even simple life forms came from outer space, transportation of some kind would be needed. And one would still have to explain how *any* life form, no matter where it came from, first came into being.

- **Creation scientists believe that the entire Bible is the Word of God, that God made the universe out of nothing,** that the Lord invented the physical laws that keep things going, and that the Creator specifically designed each plant and animal and person. Creationists differ only in how they think these things came about.

  1. *Some believe that God created everything in six literal days.* They point out that whenever the word *day* (*yom* in Hebrew) is used elsewhere in the Bible with a number in front of it—*eight* or *first*, for example—it means a literal twenty-four-hour period. Why should Genesis, chapter 1, be an exception—especially when it specifies, "...and there was evening, and there was morning—the first day"?

     References to "evening" and "morning," such as those found in the first chapter of Genesis, are used more than 100 times in the Old Testament, always with a literal meaning of a twenty-four-hour day.

     The fourth commandment states, "Six days you shall labor and do all your work. . . . For in six days the LORD made the heavens and the earth, the sea, and all that is in them, but he rested on the seventh day. Therefore the LORD blessed the Sabbath day and made it holy" (Exod. 20: 9, 11). This comparison

between the six days of creation and the six days of human la-
bor gives the impression that corresponding periods of time
are being discussed.[15]

2. *Others believe that a huge gap in time exists between Genesis 1:1
   and Genesis 1:2.* Genesis 1:1 declares: "In the beginning God
   created the heavens and the earth." Genesis 1:2 states, "Now the
   earth was [the footnote for *was* in the NIV Bible reads "or possibly *became*"] formless and empty, darkness was over the surface of the deep, and the Spirit of God was hovering over the
   waters." This verse has been interpreted to mean that there was
   an original creation and later a second creation or major revi-
   sion. It has been theorized by some that when Satan and his
   angels fell, something happened to destroy or damage the creation God first made.

3. *Another group thinks that the days in Genesis 1 refer to indefinite
   periods of time* explaining that

   In the King James Version, which most literally follows the
   Hebrew text, Genesis 2:4 reads, "These are the generations of
   the heavens and of the earth when they were created, in the day
   [Hebrew word *yom*] that the LORD God made the earth and the
   heavens." That the same author in the same work, writing on
   the same subject—Creation—uses the word *day* in a nonliteral
   sense, provides a basis for *day* in Genesis 1 not referring to
   twenty-four-hour periods.

   Day is a relative term. The length of a day on Earth, for example, is different from that on any other planet in our solar
   system. It must be remembered that the sun and the moon—
   which determine Earth days—weren't functioning until the
   fourth day of creation. Furthermore, we're told in 2 Peter 3:8,
   "With the Lord a day is like a thousand years, and a thousand
   years are like a day." Could it be that the days in the first chapter
   of Genesis were viewed from God's point of view and not from
   ours?[16]

   Some "old earth creationists" quote Psalm 90:4, which is addressed to God: "For a thousand years in your sight are like a

day that has just gone by, or like a watch in the night [three hours]." This verse forms the basis of their belief that the Earth could be very old and that if a star is twelve billion light years away, the universe is at least that old. They also believe that time had a beginning, as the Bible teaches, but they note that the Bible repeatedly says that God "stretched [or spread] out the heavens" (see Job 9:8; Ps. 104:2; Isa. 40:22; 42:5; 45:12; 48:13; 51:13; Jer. 10:12; 51:15; Zech. 12:1). They feel those are references to a "big bang creation event," which also accounts for the observation that the heavens are constantly expanding.

These aren't the only ideas credited to evolutionists or creationists—they are the most popular. But the most important issue isn't how God created the universe or how long it took Him. Rather, the most important issue is that the God of the Bible exists and has everything under His control.

BELIEVING THAT GOD ESPECIALLY DESIGNED YOU—AND EVERYTHING ELSE IN THE UNIVERSE— IS THE BASIS FOR HOPE

As you study the Bible and investigate scientific evidence, you may come to specific conclusions about Creation. But most important is not how God did it but that He created the heavens and the earth and that He made you with a special purpose in mind. That purpose includes spending eternity in heaven with Him. Knowing that you're God's masterpiece and He cares about you makes life completely worth living, even on bad days when everything seems to go wrong.

Here's what you miss out on by believing that chance, time, and naturalism enabled evolution to create everything. If the God of the Bible does not exist, then this is the best that life has to offer:

- No one loves you unconditionally and is always cheering for you.
- No one is available day and night to listen as you share your problems and how you feel about things.

- No one is wise enough to give you perfect advice.
- No way exists of finding out for sure what is right or wrong.
- No reason exists to avoid drugs, or illicit sex, or theft, or murder if you think you can escape consequences harmful to yourself.
- No reason exists to live if everything turns out wrong.
- No way exists to shake the vague feeling of guilt that keeps on surfacing.
- No hope exists that there's anything beyond death.
- The responsibility of making life worth living is yours, without any supernatural help.

Here's what you can get if you believe that God created the universe and everything in it out of nothing, and that the God of the Bible really exists:

- You have the assurance that Someone loves you unconditionally and thinks you're wonderful.
- You have the knowledge that Someone is always there—night or day—who cares and is never too busy to listen to you.
- You have a connection with Someone who has total wisdom and who is willing to share it with you.
- You have the knowledge that Someone who knows everything loves you enough to tell you how to live and what behaviors to avoid if you want a fulfilling life.
- You have the opportunity to fall in love with Someone who will give you the power to do what is right, and the motivation to please that One who loves you so much.
- You have a reason to live that is beyond yourself, and the supernatural outside help you need to cope when things go wrong.
- You have the total forgiveness for sin, and supernatural help to recover from the poor choices of the past so that you can live in freedom.
- You have the possibility of becoming rightly related to God through His Son Jesus Christ so you can spend eternity in heaven with God.

- You have the security of knowing that God's will is best for you and that the responsibility of having a life worth living is not yours alone, but can be had by following God's commandments.
- You have the knowledge that God has absolutely everything under control.

ENDNOTES

ACKNOWLEDGMENTS

1. Donald A. Bierle, *Surprised by Faith* (Lynnwood, Wash.: Emerald Books, 1992).

CHAPTER 1: MADE TO ORDER

1. Ralph O. Muncaster, *Creation Versus Evolution: New Scientific Discoveries, Investigation of the Evidence* (Mission Viejo, Calif.: Strong Basis to Believe, 1997), 22.
2. Hugh Ross, *The Creator and the Cosmos: How the Latest Scientific Discoveries Reveal God* (Colorado Springs: NavPress, 2001), 188.
3. Ibid., 189.
4. Ibid., 191.
5. Ibid., 192.
6. Ibid., 193.
7. Ibid., 187.

CHAPTER 2: UNDER CONTROL

1. Mark Littmann, Ken Willcox, and Fred Espenak, *Totality: Eclipses of the Sun* (New York: Oxford University Press, 1999), 1–40, 208–9.
2. *The New Encyclopedia Britannica: Knowledge in Depth,* s.v. "eclipse, occultation, and transit."
3. Littmann, Willcox, and Espenak, *Totality,* 1–40.

CHAPTER 3: A DEFINITION FOR "GOOD"

1. Edmund H. Harvey Jr., ed., *Reader's Digest Book of Facts* (Pleasantville, N.Y.: Reader's Digest Assoc., 1987), 299.

2. Ibid., 298.

3. *Character Sketches: From the Pages of Scripture Illustrated in the World of Nature* (Oak Brook, Ill.: Institutes in Basic Life Principles, 1985), 3:173.

4. David Louis, *2201 Fascinating Facts* (New York: Greenwich House, 1983), 213.

5. Harvey, *Reader's Digest Book of Facts,* 299.

6. Rita Thievon Mullin, *Animalogy: Weird and Wacky Animal Facts* (Bethesda, Md.: Discovery Channel Publishing; New York: Crown Publishers, 1998), 14.

7. Harvey, *Reader's Digest Book of Facts,* 286.

8. Louis, *2201 Fascinating Facts,* 10.

9. Mullin, *Animalogy,* 8.

10. Louis, *2201 Fascinating Facts,* 74.

11. Geoff Chapman, "Weird and Wonderful Seals," *Creation Ex Nihilo* 17, no. 1 (December 1994–February 1995), 36.

12. Mullin, *Animalogy,* 28.

13. Bernie Smith, *The Joy of Trivia* (Los Angeles: Brooke House, 1976), 100.

CHAPTER 4: HOPE IS SPELLED G-O-D

1. Carl Sagan quoted in Phillip E. Johnson, *Defeating Darwinism by Opening Minds* (Downers Grove, Ill.: InterVarsity, 1997), 47.

2. Stephen Hawking, *A Brief History of Time* (New York: Bantam Books, 1988), 231.

3. John D. Cutnell and Kenneth W. Johnson, *Physics* (New York: John Wiley and Sons, 1998), 95–97, 527–31, 630–34, 949–50.

4. Calculated from data in Harris Benson, *University Physics* (New York: John Wiley and Sons, 1996), 913–20.

5. Gary Parker, *Creation: Facts of Life* (Colorado Springs: Master Books, 1994), 78, 81, 83.

6. Ralph O. Muncaster, *Creation Versus Evolution: New Scientific Discoveries, Investigation of the Evidence* (Mission Viejo, Calif.: Strong Basis to Believe, 1997), 17.

CHAPTER 5: THIS WAY OUT

1. Isaac Asimov quoted in Richard A. Swenson, *More Than Meets the Eye: Fascinating Glimpses of God's Power and Design* (Colorado Springs: NavPress, 2000), 39.
2. Swenson, *More Than Meets the Eye*, 39, 40.
3. David Louis, *2201 Fascinating Facts* (New York: Greenwich House, 1983), 27.
4. Swenson, *More Than Meets the Eye*, 40.
5. Ibid., 47.
6. Ibid., 44.
7. Ibid., 51.
8. John W. Oller Jr. and John L. Omdahl, "The Origin of the Human Language Capacity: In Whose Image?" in *Creation Hypothesis: Scientific Evidence for an Intelligent Designer,* ed. J. P. Moreland (Downers Grove, Ill.: InterVarsity, 1994), 255.
9. Swenson, *More Than Meets the Eye*, 51.
10. Noam Chomsky paraphrased in Oller and Omdahl, "The Origin of the Human Language Capacity: In Whose Image?" 256.
11. Oller and Omdahl, "The Origin of the Human Language Capacity: In Whose Image?" 261.
12. Ibid., 262–66.
13. Ibid., 245–46, 248, 261.

CHAPTER 6: SOMEBODY LOVES YOU

1. Philip Yancey and Dr. Paul Brand, *Fearfully and Wonderfully Made* (Grand Rapids: Zondervan, 1987), 93.
2. Ibid., 70.
3. Richard A. Swenson, *More Than Meets the Eye: Fascinating Glimpses of God's Power and Design* (Colorado Springs: NavPress, 2000), 25-27, 89.
4. David Louis, *2201 Fascinating Facts* (New York: Greenwich House, 1983), 26.

5. Swenson, *More Than Meets the Eye,* 87.

6. Yancey and Brand, *Fearfully and Wonderfully Made,* 70.

7. Swenson, *More Than Meets the Eye,* 87–88.

8. Yancey and Brand, *Fearfully and Wonderfully Made,* 97.

9. Ann Elwood and Carol Orsay Madigan, *The Macmillan Book of Fascinating Facts: An Almanac for Kids* (New York: Macmillan, 1999), 202.

10. Swenson, *More Than Meets the Eye,* 82.

11. Elwood and Madigan, *The Macmillan Book of Fascinating Facts,* 202.

12. Swenson, *More Than Meets the Eye,* 82.

CHAPTER 7: WHO'S IN CHARGE HERE?

1. Jeffrey Bennett, Megan Donahue, Nicholas Schneider, and Mark Voit, *The Cosmic Perspective* (Menlo Park, Calif.: Addison-Wesley Longmann, 1999), 501–3.

2. David Louis, *2201 Fascinating Facts* (New York: Greenwich House, 1983), 364.

3. Ibid., 172.

4. William J. Kaufmann III and Neil F. Comins, *Discovering the Universe* (New York: W. H. Freeman and Co., 1996), 281.

5. Calculated from Harris Benson, *University Physics* (New York: John Wiley and Sons, 1996), 905.

6. Bennett, Donahue, Schneider, and Voit, *Cosmic Perspective,* 546.

7. Richard A. Swenson, *More Than Meets the Eye: Fascinating Glimpses of God's Power and Design* (Colorado Springs: NavPress, 2000), 146.

8. Bennett, Donahue, Schneider, and Voit, *Cosmic Perspective,* 503.

9. Marietta D. Moskin, *Sky Dragons and Flaming Swords: The Story of Eclipses, Comets and Other Strange Happenings in the Skies* (New York: Walker and Co., 1985), 55.

10. Bennett, Donahue, Schneider, and Voit, *Cosmic Perspective,* 349.

11. Moskin, *Sky Dragons and Flaming Swords,* 60.

12. David Wallechensky, *Twentieth Century* (Boston: Little, Brown and Co., 1995), 349.

13. Moskin, *Sky Dragons and Flaming Swords,* 60.

14. Wallechensky, *Twentieth Century,* 351.

15. Calculated from Bennett, Donahue, Schneider, and Voit, *Cosmic Perspective*, 362.

16. Wallechensky, *Twentieth Century*, 349.

17. Swenson, *More Than Meets the Eye*, 151.

18. Hugh Ross, *The Creator and the Cosmos: How the Latest Scientific Discoveries Reveal God* (Colorado Springs: NavPress, 2001), 183.

19. Calculated from Bennett, Donahue, Schneider, and Voit, *Cosmic Perspective*, 48.

20. Louis, *2201 Fascinating Facts*, 172.

21. Bernie Smith, *The Joy of Trivia* (Los Angeles: Brooke House, 1976), 178.

22. Edmund H. Harvey Jr., ed., *Reader's Digest Book of Facts* (Pleasantville, N.Y.: Reader's Digest Assoc., 1987), 397–98.

23. Calculated from Kaufmann and Comins, *Discovering the Universe*, 111.

CHAPTER 8: RUNNING GOD'S STOP SIGN

1. Gary Parker, *Creation: Facts of Life* (Colorado Springs: Master Books, 1994), 118.

2. *The World Book Encyclopedia*, s.v. "dog."

3. Ralph O. Muncaster, *Creation Versus Evolution: New Scientific Discoveries, Investigation of the Evidence* (Mission Viejo, Calif.: Strong Basis to Believe, 1997), 6.

4. *The World Book Encyclopedia*, s.v. "mule."

5. Phillip E. Johnson, *Defeating Darwinism by Opening Minds* (Downers Grove, Ill.: InterVarsity, 1997), 44.

6. Hugh Ross, *The Creator and the Cosmos: How the Latest Scientific Discoveries Reveal God* (Colorado Springs: NavPress, 2001), 141.

7. Ibid., 142.

8. Ibid., 141.

9. Paul and Ann Ehrlick quoted in ibid., 142.

10. Ross, *Creator and the Cosmos*, 142.

11. Parker, *Creation*, 72–75.

12. Jerry Bergman, "The Guppies and the Nematode," *Creation Ex Nihilo* 17, no. 1 (December 1994–February 1995): 22–23.

CHAPTER 9: LOOKING AT THE BIG PICTURE

1. *The World Book Encycopedia,* s.v. "light."
2. William J. Kaufmann III and Neil F. Comins, *Discovering the Universe* (New York: W. H. Freeman and Co., 1996), 206.
3. David Wallechensky, *Twentieth Century* (Boston: Little, Brown and Co., 1995), 365.
4. David J. Darling, *The Sun: Our Neighborhood Star* (Minneapolis, Minn.: Dillon Press, 1984), 6.
5. Jeffrey Bennett, Megan Donahue, Nicholas Schneider, and Mark Voit, *The Cosmic Perspective* (Menlo Park, Calif.: Addison-Wesley Longmann, 1999), 48.
6. David Louis, *2201 Fascinating Facts* (New York: Greenwich House, 1983), 172.
7. Bennett, Donahue, Schneider, and Voit, *Cosmic Perspective,* 9; calculation based on p. 48.
8. *The World Book Encyclopedia,* s.v. "light."
9. Hugh Ross, *The Creator and the Cosmos: How the Latest Scientific Discoveries Reveal God* (Colorado Springs: NavPress, 2001), 152, 155.
10. *The World Book Encyclopedia,* s.v. "light."
11. Richard A. Swenson, *More Than Meets the Eye: Fascinating Glimpses of God's Power and Design* (Colorado Springs: NavPress, 2000), 176.
12. Calculated from James B. Kaler, *Astronomy* (New York: Harper Collins, 1994), 125; and Bennet, Donahue, Schneider, and Voit, *Cosmic Perspective,* 164, 165.
13. Calculated from Harris Benson, *University Physics* (New York: John Wiley and Sons, 1996), inside front cover.
14. Swenson, *More Than Meets the Eye,* 174.

CHAPTER 10: GETTING IT ALL TOGETHER

1. Richard A. Swenson, *More Than Meets the Eye: Fascinating Glimpses of God's Power and Design* (Colorado Springs: NavPress, 2000), 79–81.
2. Swenson, 81.
3. Philip Yancey and Paul Brand, *Fearfully and Wonderfully Made* (Grand Rapids: Zondervan, 1987), 154.

4. Yancey and Brand, *Fearfully and Wonderfully Made,* 152, 153.

5. Swenson, *More Than Meets the Eye,* 80.

6. Yancey and Brand, *Fearfully and Wonderfully Made,* 125.

7. Ibid., 118, 125.

8. Swenson, *More Than Meets the Eye,* 80.

CHAPTER 11: GOD'S GOT YOU COVERED

1. Richard A. Swenson, *More Than Meets the Eye: Fascinating Glimpses of God's Power and Design* (Colorado Springs: NavPress, 2000), 34.

2. Ibid., 32.

3. Ibid.

4. Ibid., 32–34.

5. Ibid., 33, 34.

6. Philip Yancey and Paul Brand, *Fearfully and Wonderfully Made* (Grand Rapids: Zondervan, 1987), 22.

7. Swenson, *More Than Meets the Eye,* 34.

8. Ibid.

9. Yancey and Brand, *Fearfully and Wonderfully Made,* 188.

CHAPTER 12: THE UNIVERSE HAS A DIRECTOR

1. Hugh Ross, *The Creator and the Cosmos: How the Latest Scientific Discoveries Reveal God* (Colorado Springs: NavPress, 2001), 32.

2. David Louis, *2201 Fascinating Facts* (New York: Greenwich House, 1983), 362.

3. Marietta D. Moskin, *Sky Dragons and Flaming Swords: The Story of Eclipses, Comets and Other Strange Happenings in the Skies* (New York: Walker and Co., 1985), 54.

4. Richard A. Swenson, *More Than Meets the Eye: Fascinating Glimpses of God's Power and Design* (Colorado Springs: NavPress, 2000), 152–53.

5. Edmund H. Harvey Jr., *Reader's Digest Book of Facts* (Pleasantville, N.Y.: Reader's Digest Assoc., 1987), 399.

6. James B. Kaler, *Astronomy* (New York: Harper Collins, 1994), 198–99.

7. Harvey, *Reader's Digest Book of Facts,* 390.

8. Kaler, *Astronomy,* 230.

9. Ross, *Creator and the Cosmos,* 181.

10. Ibid., 210.

11. Ibid., 210, 211.

12. "The Milky Way Galaxy: A spiral galaxy, type Sbc, centered in Sagittarius" http://www.seds.org/messier/more/mn.html (accessed November 5, 2003).

13. Louis, *2201 Fascinating Facts,* 172.

14. Jeffrey Bennett, Megan Donahue, Nicholas Schneider, and Mark Voit, *The Cosmic Perspective* (Menlo Park, Calif.: Addison-Wesley Longmann, 1999), 535.

15. CNN.com/SCIENCE & SPACE, "Star survey reaches 70 sextillion," 23, July 2003 http://www.cnn.com/2003/TECH/space/07/22/stars.survey (accessed November 5, 2003).

16. *The World Book Encyclopedia,* s.v. "elements."

17. L. Berkhof, *Manual of Christian Doctrine* (Grand Rapids: Eerdmans, 1965), 63.

CHAPTER 13: PLUG INTO GOD'S SYSTEM

1. Kurt P. Wise, "The Origin of Life's Major Groups," in *Creation Hypothesis: Scientific Evidence for an Intelligent Designer,* ed. J. P. Moreland (Downers Grove, Ill.: InterVarsity, 1994), 229.

2. Bernie Smith, *The Joy of Trivia* (Los Angeles: Brooke House, 1976), 98.

3. *Reader's Digest Facts and Fallacies: Stories of the Strange and the Unusual* (Pleasantville, N.Y.: Reader's Digest Assoc., 1988), 55.

4. Charis Conn and Ilena Silverman, eds., *What Counts: The Complete Harper's Index* (New York: Holt, 1991), 142.

5. Smith, *Joy of Trivia,* 228.

6. Edmund H. Harvey Jr., ed., *Reader's Digest Book of Facts* (Pleasantville, N.Y.: Reader's Digest Assoc., 1987), 295.

7. Wise, "The Origin of Life's Major Groups," 229.

8. Gary Parker, *Creation: Facts of Life* (Colorado Springs: Master Books, 1994), 78–79.

9. Ibid.

CHAPTER 14: AUTOMATIC LIVING

1. Philip Yancey and Paul Brand, *Fearfully and Wonderfully Made* (Grand Rapids: Zondervan, 1987), 164–65, 169.

2. Richard A. Swenson, *More Than Meets the Eye: Fascinating Glimpses of God's Power and Design* (Colorado Springs: NavPress, 2000), 29.

3. David Louis, *2201 Fascinating Facts* (New York: Greenwich House, 1983), 27.

4. Swenson, *More Than Meets the Eye*, 29.

5. Louis, *2201 Fascinating Facts*, 26.

6. Yancey and Brand, *Fearfully and Wonderfully Made*, 169–70.

7. Swenson, *More Than Meets the Eye*, 24; Louis, *2201 Fascinating Facts*, 27.

8. Swenson, *More Than Meets the Eye*, 23.

9. Louis, *2201 Fascinating Facts*, 220.

10. Swenson, *More Than Meets the Eye*, 23.

11. Louis, *2201 Fascinating Facts*, 221.

12. Swenson, *More Than Meets the Eye*, 85–87.

CHAPTER 15: FEAR-BUSTING INFORMATION

1. D. James Kennedy, *Why I Believe in God* (Ft. Lauderdale, Fla.: Coral Ridge Ministries), 5–7.

2. Hugh Ross, *The Creator and the Cosmos: How the Latest Scientific Discoveries Reveal God* (Colorado Springs: NavPress, 2001), 184.

3. Ibid., 185, 186.

4. From the web site of the California and Carnegie Planet Search: www.exoplanets.org, (accessed October 6, 2003).

5. Ross, *Creator and the Cosmos*, 186.

6. Ibid., 175–85.

7. Ibid., 187.

8. Ibid., 198–99.

CHAPTER 16: YOU'RE NOT MISSING A THING

1. Richard A. Swenson, *More Than Meets the Eye: Fascinating Glimpses of God's Power and Design* (Colorado Springs: NavPress, 2000), 17.

2. Calculated from ibid., and Bernie Smith, *The Joy of Trivia* (Los Angeles: Brook House, 1976), 180.

3. Swenson, *More Than Meets the Eye*, 20.

4. Ibid., 20–21.

5. Ibid., 20.

6. Ibid., 83.

7. Ibid., 20.

8. Ibid., 17.

9. Ibid., 18.

10. David M. Bougham quoted in ibid., 18.

11. Sir J. Arthur Thomson quoted in ibid., 18.

12. Ibid., 18.

13. John Tyndall quoted in ibid., 18.

14. Peter Kreeft and Ronald K. Tacelli, *Handbook of Christian Apologetics* (Downers Grove, Ill: InterVarsity, 1994), 50.

CHAPTER 17: GETTING BACK ON TRACK

1. D. James Kennedy, *Why I Believe in God* (Ft. Lauderdale, Fla.: Coral Ridge Ministries), 5.

2. "Visit to an Ocean Planet, http://topex-www.;pl.nasa.gov/education/activities/t5355ac3pdf, (accessed October 15, 2003).

3. Kennedy, *Why I Believe in God*, 5.

4. Hugh Ross, *The Creator and the Cosmos: How the Latest Scientific Discoveries Reveal God* (Colorado Springs: NavPress, 2001), 192.

5. Mark Littmann, Ken Willcox, and Fred Espenak, *Totality: Eclipses of the Sun* (New York: Oxford University Press, 1999), 9.

6. Calculated from William J. Kaufmann III and Neil F. Comins, *Discovering the Universe* (New York: W. H. Freeman and Co., 1996), 396.

7. Littmann, Willcox, and Espenak, *Totality*, 9, 11.

8. William J. Kaufmann III, *Universe* (New York: W. H. Freeman and Co., 1994), 164.

CHAPTER 18: HAVE IT GOD'S WAY

1. Gary Parker, *Creation: Facts of Life* (Colorado Springs: Master Books, 1994), 118, 120.

2. *Amazing Animals of Australia* (Washington, D.C.: National Geographic Society, 1984), 72.

3. *Reader's Digest Facts and Fallacies: Stories of the Strange and the Unusual* (Pleasantville, N.Y.: Reader's Digest Assoc., 1988), 61.

4. *Amazing Animals of Australia,* 72.

5. "Poisonous Mammals," http: //www.cs.bris.ac.uk/~nt0723/ mammals.html (accessed June 20, 2002).

6. *The World Book Encyclopedia,* s.v. "platypus."

7. "Poisonous Mammals," http://www.cs.bris.ac.uk/~nt0723/mammals. html (accessed June 20, 2002).

8. Richard A. Swenson, *More Than Meets the Eye: Fascinating Glimpses of God's Power and Design* (Colorado Springs: NavPress, 2000), 26.

9. Using information from Fred Heeren cited in ibid., 26.

10. Parker, *Creation,* 44.

11. Swenson, *More Than Meets the Eye,* 32.

12. Edmund H. Harvey Jr., ed., *Reader's Digest Book of Facts* (Pleasantville, N.Y.: Reader's Digest Assoc., 1987), 298.

13. Parker, *Creation,* 44–45.

14. Harvey, *Reader's Digest Book of Facts,* 281.

CHAPTER 19: DON'T MISS OUT ON MIRACLES

1. Richard A. Swenson, *More Than Meets the Eye: Fascinating Glimpses of God's Power and Design* (Colorado Springs: NavPress, 2000), 53.

2. David Louis, *2201 Fascinating Facts* (New York: Greenwich House, 1983), 9.

3. Swenson, *More Than Meets the Eye,* 53.

4. Louis, *2201 Fascinating Facts,* 7.

5. Edmund H. Harvey Jr., ed., *Reader's Digest Book of Facts* (Pleasantville, N.Y.: Reader's Digest Assoc., 1987), 266.

6. Bernie Smith, *The Joy of Trivia* (Los Angeles: Brooke House, 1976), 229.

7. Kurt P. Wise, "The Origin of Life's Major Groups," in *Creation Hypothesis: Scientific Evidence for an Intelligent Designer,* ed. J. P. Moreland (Downers Grove, Ill.: InterVarsity, 1994), 228.

8. Harvey, *Reader's Digest Book of Facts,* 302.

9. Ibid.

10. Ibid.

11. Ibid.

12. *Character Sketches: From the Pages of Scripture Illustrated in the World of Nature* (Oak Brook, Ill.: Institutes in Basic Life Principles, 1985), 1:204.

CHAPTER 20: YOUR LIFE HAS A SPECIAL PURPOSE

1. Richard A. Swenson, *More Than Meets the Eye: Fascinating Glimpses of God's Power and Design* (Colorado Springs: NavPress, 2000), 70.

2. Ralph O. Muncaster, *Creation Versus Evolution: New Scientific Discoveries, Investigation of the Evidence* (Mission Viejo, Calif.: Strong Basis to Believe, 1997), 20.

3. Peter Stoner, author of *Science Speaks* (Wheaton, Ill.: Van Kampen, 1952), quoted in Josh McDowell, *Evidence That Demands a Verdict: Historical Evidence for the Christian Faith* (San Bernardino, Calif.: Here's Life Publishers, 1992), 1:167.

4. Charis Conn and Ilena Silverman, eds., *What Counts: The Complete Harper's Index* (New York: Holt, 1991), 138.

5. Hugh Ross, *The Creator and the Cosmos: How the Latest Scientific Discoveries Reveal God* (Colorado Springs: NavPress, 2001), 153.

6. Muncaster, *Creation Versus Evolution*, 20.

7. Ibid.

8. Gary Parker, *Creation: Facts of Life* (Colorado Springs: Master Books, 1994), 33–34.

9. Swenson, *More Than Meets the Eye*, 69–70.

10. Ibid., 71.

CHAPTER 21: BEATING BOREDOM

1. *The World Book Encyclopedia*, s.v. "water."

2. James Kennedy, *Why I Believe in God* (Ft. Lauderdale, Fla.: Coral Ridge Ministries), 7–8.

3. "Mixtures and Solutions," http://www.utdallas.edu/dept/sci_ed/BarbaraP5501/Mixtures%20and%20Solutions.doc, (accessed October 15, 2003).

4. *The World Book Encyclopedia*, s.v. "water."

5. James Kennedy, *Why I Believe in God*, 7.

6. Hugh Ross, *The Creator and the Cosmos: How the Latest Scientific Discoveries Reveal God* (Colorado Springs: NavPress, 2001), 191.

7. Kennedy, *Why I Believe in God*, 7.

8. *The World Book Encyclopedia*, s.v. "water."

9. Ross, *Creator and the Cosmos*, 156

10. "Snowflakes," n.a., *Creation Ex Nihilo* 17, no.1 (December 1994–February 1995): 26–27.

11. Walter L. Bradley and Charles B. Thaxton, "Information and the Origin of Life," in *Creation Hypothesis: Scientific Evidence for an Intelligent Designer*, ed. J. P. Moreland (Downers Grove, Ill.: InterVarsity, 1994), 195–203.

12. Richard A. Swenson, *More Than Meets the Eye: Fascinating Glimpses of God's Power and Design* (Colorado Springs: NavPress, 2000), 68.

CHAPTER 22:   WEAPONS FOR WINNING

1. *Character Sketches: From the Pages of Scripture Illustrated in the World of Nature* (Oak Brook, Ill.: Institutes in Basic Life Principles, 1985), 3:347.

2. Bernie Smith, *The Joy of Trivia* (Los Angeles: Brooke House, 1976), 118.

3. Gary Parker, *Creation: Facts of Life* (Colorado Springs: Master Books, 1994), 79–80.

4. Edmund H. Harvey Jr., ed., *Reader's Digest Book of Facts* (Pleasantville, N.Y.: Reader's Digest Assoc., 1987), 297.

5. Ibid., 296.

6. *The World Book Encyclopedia*, s.v. "lizard."

7. Harvey, *Reader's Digest Book of Facts*, 296.

8. *Character Sketches*, 1:142.

9. Harvey, *Reader's Digest Book of Facts*, 295.

10. Ibid., 296.

11. Ibid., 290.

12. *Character Sketches*, 1:83.

13. Ibid., 1:366, 371.

14. Ibid., 1:172.

15. Ibid., 1:357.

16. Smith, *Joy of Trivia*, 229.

CHAPTER 23:   INSULATION AGAINST FUTURE SHOCK

1. Gary Parker, *Creation: Facts of Life* (Colorado Springs: Master Books, 1994), 58–59.

2. Ibid., 59.

3. Ibid., 58–59.

CHAPTER 24:   FOREVER HOPE

1. Stephen Hawking, *A Brief History of Time* (New York: Bantam Books, 1988), 184.

2. Hugh Ross, *The Creator and the Cosmos: How the Latest Scientific Discoveries Reveal God* (Colorado Springs: NavPress, 2001), 26.

3. Richard A. Swenson, *More Than Meets the Eye: Fascinating Glimpses of God's Power and Design* (Colorado Springs: NavPress, 2000), 121-31.

4. David Louis, *2201 Fascinating Facts* (New York: Greenwich House, 1983), 13.

5. Charis Conn and Ilena Silverman, eds., *What Counts: The Complete Harper's Index* (New York: Holt, 1991), 141.

6. Ross, *Creator and the Cosmos*, 142.

7. Gary Parker, *Creation: Facts of Life* (Colorado Springs: Master Books, 1994), 138.

8. Ross, *Creator and the Cosmos*, 116.

9. Swenson, *More Than Meets the Eye*, 121–31.

10. Ibid., 126.

CHAPTER 25:   CUSTOM-MADE BY AN AWESOME CREATOR

1. Rita Thievon Mullin, *Animalogy: Weird and Wacky Animal Facts* (Bethesda, Md.: Discovery Channel Publishing; New York: Crown Publishers, 1998), 55.

2. Charis Conn and Ilena Silverman, eds., *What Counts: The Complete Harper's Index* (New York: Holt, 1991), 142.

3. Sylvia A. Johnson, *Penguins: A Lerner Science Book* (Minneapolis, Minn., Lerner Publications, 1981), 5, 32.

4. *The World Book Encyclopedia*, s.v. "penguin."

5. Christopher M. Perkins and Alex L. A. Middleton, *The Encyclopedia of Birds* (New York: Facts on File Publications, 1985), 38.

6. *Character Sketches: From the Pages of Scripture Illustrated in the World of Nature* (Oak Brook, Ill.: Institutes in Basic Life Principles, 1985), 1:292.

7. Mullin, *Animalogy*, 54.

8. Jane R. McCauley, *Africa's Animal Giants* (Washington, D.C.: National Geographic Society, 1987), 5.

9. *The World Book Encyclopedia*, s.v. "camel."

10. Alexander Parsons, *Amazing Mammals* (New York: Alfred A. Knopf, 1988), 13.

11. Edmund H. Harvey Jr., ed., *Reader's Digest Book of Facts* (Pleasantville, N.Y.: Reader's Digest Assoc., 1987), 283.

12. *Character Sketches*, 3:172.

13. Ibid., 2:30.

14. David Louis, *2201 Fascinating Facts* (New York: Greenwich House, 1983), 14.

15. *The World Book Encyclopedia*, s.v. "chameleon."

16. Mullin, *Animalogy*, 52.

17. Phillip E. Johnson, *Defeating Darwinism by Opening Minds* (Downers Grove, Ill.: InterVarsity, 1997), 59.

18. Ibid.

19. Gary Parker, *Creation: Facts of Life* (Colorado Springs: Master Books, 1994), 56.

20. Helen Lemmel, "Turn Your Eyes upon Jesus," public domain.

CHAPTER 26: HE'S PERFECT—THAT IS GOD

1. *The World Book Encyclopedia*, s.v. "redwood."

2. David Louis, *2201 Fascinating Facts* (New York: Greenwich House, 1983), 258.

3. Ibid., 57.

4. "The Giant Sequoia—Forest Masterpiece," http://sequoia.areaparks.com/parkinformation.html?content=bigtrees, (accessed March 12, 2004).

5. Bernie Smith, *The Joy of Trivia* (Los Angeles: Brooke House, 1976), 234.

6. "The Giant Sequoia—Forest Masterpiece," http://sequoia.areaparks.com/parkinformation.html?content=bigtrees, (accessed March 12, 2004).

7. Ginger Wadsworth, *Giant Sequoia Trees* (Minneapolis, Minn.: Lerner Publishing, 1995), 10.

8. *The World Book Encyclopedia*, s.v. "sequoia."

9. Louis, *2201 Fascinating Facts*, 56.

10. *Character Sketches: From the Pages of Scripture Illustrated in the World of Nature* (Oak Brook, Ill..: Institutes in Basic Life Principles, 1985), 3:161.

11. Smith, *Joy of Trivia*, 225.

12. *The World Book Encyclopedia*, s.v. "bamboo."

13. Smith, *Joy of Trivia*, 237.

14. *The World Book Encyclopedia*, s.v. "bamboo."

15. Charis Conn and Ilena Silverman, eds., *What Counts: The Complete Harper's Index* (New York: Holt, 1991), 138.

16. *The World Book Encyclopedia*, s.v. "soybean."

17. Smith, *Joy of Trivia*, 235.

CHAPTER 27: THE WORLD YOU CREATE WILL FALL APART

1. Gary Parker, *Creation: Facts of Life* (Colorado Springs: Master Books, 1994), 89, 91.

2. Ibid., 89, 92.

3. Ibid., 93.

4. Ibid.

5. Ibid.

6. Ralph O. Muncaster, *Creation Versus Evolution: New Scientific Discoveries, Investigation of the Evidence* (Mission Viejo, Calif.: Strong Basis to Believe, 1997), 6.

7. Parker, *Creation*, 92.

8. Carl Wieland, "Beetle Bloopers," *Creation* (No City: Genesis Ministries International, 1997), June–August, 19(3):30.
9. Parker, *Creation*, 98.
10. Ibid., 99.
11. Muncaster, *Creation Versus Evolution*, 12.

CHAPTER 28: THE BIG IMPACT OF LITTLE THINGS

1. Ralph O. Muncaster, *Creation Versus Evolution: New Scientific Discoveries, Investigation of the Evidence* (Mission Viejo, Calif.: Strong Basis to Believe, 1997), 16.
2. Richard A. Swenson, *More Than Meets the Eye: Fascinating Glimpses of God's Power and Design* (Colorado Springs: NavPress, 2000), 19, 20.
3. Hugh Ross, *The Creator and the Cosmos: How the Latest Scientific Discoveries Reveal God* (Colorado Springs: NavPress, 2001), 143.
4. Mark Calwell, "The Clock in the Cell," *Discover,* Oct. 1998: 36.
5. Rosevear in Swenson, *More Than Meets the Eye*, 21.
6. Richard Dawking quoted in Phillip E. Johnson, *Defeating Darwinism by Opening Minds* (Downers Grove, Ill.: InterVarsity, 1997), 77.
7. Swenson, *More Than Meets the Eye*, 21.
8. *The World Book Encyclopedia*, s.v. "cell."
9. David Rosevear, "The Myth of Chemical Evolution," *Impact,* July 1999 iv, quoted in Swenson, *More Than Meets the Eye*, 21.
10. Swenson, *More Than Meets the Eye*, 21, 25, 26.

CHAPTER 29: LIVING ABOVE IT ALL

1. *Character Sketches: From the Pages of Scripture Illustrated in the World of Nature* (Oak Brook, Ill.: Institutes in Basic Life Principles, 1985), 1:296.
2. Joanna Cule, *A Bird's Body* (New York: William Morrow and Co., 1982), 12.
3. Rita Thievon Mullin, *Animalogy: Weird and Wacky Animal Facts* (Bethesda, Md.: Discovery Channel Publishing; New York: Crown Publishers, 1998), 7.
4. Cule, *A Bird's Body*, 20, 30.

5. Bernie Smith, *The Joy of Trivia* (Los Angeles: Brooke House, 1976), 103.

6. Cule, *A Bird's Body,* 32–36.

7. Philip Yancey and Paul Brand, *Fearfully and Wonderfully Made* (Grand Rapids: Zondervan, 1987), 165.

8. Cule, *A Bird's Body,* 36.

9. Mullin, *Animalogy,* 28.

10. Cule, *A Bird's Body,* 5.

11. Gary Parker, *Creation: Facts of Life* (Colorado Springs: Master Books, 1994), 148–55.

CHAPTER 30: FINDING SOME ANSWERS

1. Richard A. Swenson, *More Than Meets the Eye: Fascinating Glimpses of God's Power and Design* (Colorado Springs: NavPress, 2000), 61.

2. Gary Parker, *Creation: Facts of Life* (Colorado Springs: Master Books, 1994), 24, 29–30.

3. Ibid., 29.

4. Ibid., 32.

5. Hugh Ross, *The Creator and the Cosmos: How the Latest Scientific Discoveries Reveal God* (Colorado Springs: NavPress, 2001), 207.

6. Ibid.

7. Swenson, *More Than Meets the Eye,* 62–65.

8. Ibid., 65.

9. Michael Behe quoted in ibid., 65.

10. Swenson, *More Than Meets the Eye,* 62–65.

11. Ibid., 64.

12. Carl Wieland, "The Marvelous Messenger Molecule," *Creation Ex Nihilo,* Sept.–Nov. 1995: 17(4) 10–13.

13. Phillip E. Johnson, *Defeating Darwinism by Opening Minds* (Downers Grove, Ill.: InterVarsity, 1997), 73.

14. Swenson, *More Than Meets the Eye,* 67.

15. Ibid., 66.

CHAPTER 31: GOD: UP CLOSE AND PERSONAL

1. E. C. Knupp, *The Rainbow and You* (New York: Harper Collins, 2000), 29.

2. Ibid., 7–28.

3. *Reader's Digest Facts and Fallacies: Stories of the Strange and the Unusual* (Pleasantville, N.Y.: Reader's Digest Assoc., 1988), 28.

4. A. B. C. Whipple, *Storm* (Alexandria, Va.: Time-Life Book, 1982), 119.

5. Whipple, *Storm*, 127.

6. Charis Conn and Ilena Silverman, eds., *What Counts: The Complete Harper's Index* (New York: Holt, 1991), 137.

7. Peter Viemeister, *The Lightning Book* (Boston: MIT Press, 1972), 122.

8. Ibid., 225.

9. Calculated from ibid.

10. Robert Greenler, *Rainbows, Halos and Glories* (Cambridge, England: Cambridge University Press, 1980), 5.

11. Ideas from C. D. Watson quoted in W. A. Pratney, *The Nature and Character of God* (Minneapolis, Minn.: Bethany House, 1988), 114.

CONCLUSION: DECIDING HOW TO VIEW YOUR WORLD

1. *The World Book Encyclopedia*, s.v. "evolution."

2. Phillip E. Johnson, *Defeating Darwinism by Opening Minds* (Downers Grove, Ill.: InterVarsity, 1997), 15.

3. George Gaylord Simpson quoted in ibid.

4. Johnson, *Defeating Darwinism*, 16.

5. Gary Parker, *Creation: Facts of Life* (Colorado Springs: Master Books, 1994), 86–88.

6. Ken Ham, codirector of Creation Science ministries, interviewed on "Truths That Transform" and summarized in an *Action Sheet* (Ft. Lauderdale, Fla.: Truths That Transform, 6 December 1994), 2.

7. Ibid.

8. *Encyclopedia Americana*, s.v. "piltdown hoax."

9. Ham, codirector of Creation Science ministries, interviewed on "Truths That Transform" and summarized in an *Action Sheet*, 2.

10. Parker, *Creation*, 98.

11. Ibid., 99.

12. Ibid.

13. Ibid., 98.

14. James Strong, *Strong's Exhaustive Concordance of the Bible* (Nashville: Abingdons, 1980).

15. Information from CRI statement DA060 *Age of Creation* (P.O. Box 7000, Rancho Santa Margarota, CA 92688), 1a–c, 2a–b.

16. Ibid.